The Professional Programmers Guide to
Fortran 77

The Professional Programmers Guide to

Fortran 77

Clive G Page
Department of Physics
University of Leicester

Pitman

PITMAN PUBLISHING
128 Long Acre, London WC2E 9AN

© Clive G Page 1988

First published in Great Britain 1988

British Library Cataloguing in Publication Data
Page, Clive
 The professional programmers guide to
 Fortran 77. — (Professional programmers
 guides).
 1. FORTRAN (Computer program language)
 1. Title
 005.13'3   QA76.73.F25

ISBN 0 273 02856 1

All rights reserved; no part of this publication may be reproduced, stored in a retrieval system, or transmitted in any form or by any means, electronic, mechanical, photocopying, recording, or otherwise without either the prior written permission of the publishers or a licence permitting restricted copying issued by the copyright Licensing Agency Ltd, 33–34 Alfred Place, London, WC1E 7DP. This book may not be lent, resold, hired out or otherwise disposed of by way of trade in any form of binding or cover other than that in which it is published, without the prior consent of the publishers.

Printed and bound in Great Britain at
The Bath Press, Avon

Contents

Preface ix

1 **What is Fortran? 1**
    1.1   Early development 1
    1.2   Standardisation 2
    1.3   Strengths and weaknesses 3
    1.4   Precautions 4

2 **Basic Fortran Concepts 7**
    2.1   Statements 7
    2.2   Expressions and assignments 8
    2.3   Integer and real data types 10
    2.4   DO-loops 11
    2.5   Formatted output 12
    2.6   Functions 13
    2.7   IF-blocks 14
    2.8   Arrays 15

3 **Fortran in Practice 18**
    3.1   The Fortran system 18
    3.2   Creating the source code 20
    3.3   Compiling 21
    3.4   Linking 22
    3.5   Program development 23

4 **Program Structure and Layout 26**
    4.1   The Fortran character set 26
    4.2   Statements and lines 27
    4.3   Program units 30
    4.4   Statement types and order 32
    4.5   Symbolic names 33
    4.6   PROGRAM statement 35
    4.7   END statement 35

5 **Constants, Variables and Arrays 37**
    5.1   Data types 37

5.2 Constants 42
  5.3 Specifying data type 45
  5.4 Named constants 48
  5.5 Variables 51
  5.6 Arrays 52

6 **Arithmetic 55**
  6.1 Arithmetic expressions 55
  6.2 Arithmetic intrinsic functions 61
  6.3 Arithmetic assignment statements 65

7 **Character Handling and Logic 67**
  7.1 Character facilities 67
  7.2 Character substrings 68
  7.3 Character expressions 69
  7.4 Character assignment statements 70
  7.5 Character intrinsic functions 71
  7.6 Relational expressions 73
  7.7 Logical expressions 76
  7.8 Logical assignment statements 78

8 **Control Statements 79**
  8.1 Control structures 79
  8.2 IF-blocks 80
  8.3 DO-loops 82
  8.4 Logical-IF statement 85
  8.5 Unconditional GO TO statement 85
  8.6 Computed GO TO statement 86
  8.7 STOP statement 87

9 **Procedures 89**
  9.1 Intrinsic functions 89
  9.2 Statement functions 90
  9.3 External procedures 93
  9.4 Arguments of external procedures 96
  9.5 Variables as dummy arguments 98
  9.6 Arrays as arguments 101
  9.7 Procedures as arguments 104
  9.8 SUBROUTINE and CALL statements 106
  9.9 RETURN statement 107
  9.10 FUNCTION statement 108
  9.11 SAVE statement 110
  9.12 EXTERNAL and INTRINSIC statements 111

10 Input/Output Facilities 113
- 10.1 Files, I/O units and records 113
- 10.2 External files 117
- 10.3 Internal files 120
- 10.4 Pre-connected files 122
- 10.5 Error and end-of-file conditions 123
- 10.6 Format specifications 125
- 10.7 Format edit descriptors 127
- 10.8 Format data descriptors 128
- 10.9 Format control descriptors 132
- 10.10 List-directed formatting 135
- 10.11 Carriage-control and printing 137
- 10.12 Input/output statements and keywords 138
- 10.13 OPEN statement 139
- 10.14 CLOSE statement 142
- 10.15 INQUIRE statement 142
- 10.16 READ and WRITE statements 145
- 10.17 REWIND and BACKSPACE statements 148

11 The DATA Statement 150
- 11.1 Defined and undefined values 150
- 11.2 Initialising variables 151
- 11.3 Initialising arrays 152
- 11.4 DATA statements in procedures 153
- 11.5 General rules 154

12 Common Blocks 156
- 12.1 Using common blocks 156
- 12.2 Blank common blocks 161
- 12.3 COMMON statement 162
- 12.4 Block data program units 162

Appendix A: Obsolete and Deprecated Features 164

Appendix B: Summary of Subset Differences 170

Appendix C: List of Intrinsic Functions 172

Index 175

Preface

This Guide provides concise but complete descriptions of all the features of current Fortran. The depth of treatment is suitable for the serious or professional programmer, but the introductory sections assume no previous knowledge of the language. Each topic is fully illustrated with examples of Fortran programs.

Fortran is the most widely used language in the world for scientific and numerical computing. The first chapter gives a brief account of its history and future prospects followed by a discussion of its current strengths and weaknesses. Chapter 2 uses a series of carefully graded examples to introduce the basic elements of Fortran to the new user. Chapter 3 explains how the Fortran compiler and linker are used to translate a source program into executable form. In the remaining chapters each aspect of the Fortran language is described in detail with the aid of numerous programming examples.

The emphasis throughout is on the creation of well-structured programs which are robust, portable, efficient and easy to maintain. Each chapter contains suggestions and guidelines which will help programmers of all levels of experience to produce Fortran programs of the highest quality.

The language covered here is that of the latest official standard (ANSI X3.9–1978 and ISO 1539–1980). The only forms of statement not covered in the main part of the text are those which are obsolete or generally regarded as unsatisfactory. These forms, retained in the language mainly for compatibility with older software, are covered briefly in Appendix A.

1 What is Fortran?

Fortran is the most widely used programming language in the world for numerical applications. It has achieved this position partly by being on the scene earlier than any of the other major languages and partly because it seems gradually to have evolved the features which its users, especially scientists and engineers, found most useful. In order to retain compatibility with old programs, Fortran has advanced mainly by adding new features rather than by removing old ones. The net result is, of course, that some parts of the language are, by present standards, rather archaic: some of these can be avoided easily, others can still be a nuisance.

This chapter gives a brief history of the language, outlines its future prospects, and summarises its strengths and weaknesses.

1.1 Early Development

Fortran was invented by a team of programmers working for IBM in the early 1950s. This group, led by John Backus, produced the first compiler, for an IBM 704 computer, in 1957. They used the name Fortran because one of their principal aims was 'formula translation'. But Fortran was in fact one of the very first high-level languages: it came complete with control structures and facilities for input/output. Fortran became popular quite rapidly and compilers were soon produced for other IBM machines. Before long, other manufacturers were forced to design Fortran compilers for their own hardware. By 1963 all the major manufacturers had joined in and there were dozens of different Fortran compilers in existence, many of them rather more powerful than the original.

All this resulted in a chaos of incompatible dialects. Some order was restored in 1966 when an American national standard was defined for Fortran. This was the first time that a standard had ever been produced for a computer programming language. Although it was very valuable, it hardly checked the growth of the language. Quite deliberately the Fortran 66 standard only specified a set of language features which had to be present: it did not prevent other features being added. As time went on these extensions proliferated and the need for a further standardisation exercise became apparent. This eventually resulted in the current version of the language: Fortran 77.

1.2 Standardisation

One of the most important features of Fortran programs is their *portability*, that is the ease with which they can be moved from one computer system to another. Now that each generation of hardware succeeds the previous one every few years, while good software often lasts for much longer, more and more programs need to be portable. The growth in computer networks is also encouraging the development of portable programs.

The first step in achieving portability is to ensure that a standard form of programming language is acceptable everywhere. This need is now widely recognised and has resulted in the development of standards for all the major programming languages. In practice, however, many of the new standards have been ignored and standard-conforming systems for languages like BASIC and Pascal are still very rare.

Fortunately, Fortran is in much better shape: almost all current Fortran systems are designed to conform to the standard usually called Fortran 77. This was produced in 1977 by a committee of the American National Standards Institute (ANSI) and was subsequently adopted by the International Standards Organisation (ISO). The definition was published as ANSI X3.9-1978 and ISO 1539-1980. The term 'Standard Fortran' will be used in the rest of this book to mean Fortran 77 according to this definition.

Fortran is now one of the most widely used computer languages in the world with compilers available for almost every type of computer on the market. Since Fortran 77 is quite good at handling character strings as well as numbers, and also has powerful file-handling and input/output facilities, it is suitable for a much wider range of applications than before.

Full and subset Fortran

The ANSI Standard actually defines two different levels for Fortran 77. The simpler form, *subset* Fortran, was intended for use on computers which were too small to handle the *full* language. Now that even personal computers are powerful enough to handle full Fortran 77, subset Fortran is practically obsolete. This book, therefore, only describes full Fortran 77. The features which do not need to be provided in systems which only conform to the subset are summarised in Appendix B.

Fortran 8x

Considerable progress has been made on the design of the next Fortran standard, provisionally called Fortran 8x. The ANSI and ISO committees have decided to bring Fortran right up to date by removing as many restrictions as possible and adopting a large number of new features, many of them already in use in other high-level languages.

Unfortunately these changes are so radical that they have encountered considerable opposition, especially from some of the major computer manufacturers. Because of this controversy, it seems increasingly unlikely that compilers to the new standard will appear before the early 1990s. The current intention is that the new Fortran standard (whatever it is called) will contain the whole of Fortran 77 as a subset, so that existing programs can continue in use without alteration.

Fortran has already survived competition from Algol-60, PL/1, and Algol-68 (while adopting a few of their best features); the improvements planned for Fortran 8x mean that it is likely to continue in use well into the next century. It may well outlive Pascal, leaving Ada as the only serious challenger.

1.3 Strengths and Weaknesses

Fortran has become popular and widespread because of its unique combination of properties. Its numerical and input/output facilities are almost unrivalled while those for logic and character handling are as good as most other languages. Fortran is simple enough that you do not need to be a computer specialist to become familiar with it fairly quickly, yet it has features, such as the independent compilation of program units, which allow it to be used on very large applications. Programs written in Fortran are also more portable than those in other major languages. The efficiency of compiled code also tends to be quite high because the language is straightforward to compile and techniques for handling Fortran have reached a considerable degree of refinement. Finally, the ease with which existing procedures can be incorporated into new software makes it especially easy to develop new programs out of old ones.

It cannot be denied, however, that Fortran has more than its fair share of weaknesses and drawbacks. Many of these have existed in Fortran since it was first invented and ought to have been eliminated long ago: examples include the 6-character limit on symbolic names, the fixed statement layout, and the need to use statement labels.

Fortran also has rather liberal rules and an extensive system of default values: while this reduces programming effort it also makes it harder for the system to detect the programmer's mistakes. In many other programming languages, for example, the data type of every variable has to be declared in advance. Fortran does not insist on this but, in consequence, if you make a spelling mistake in a variable name the compiler is likely to use two variables when you only intended to use one. Such errors can be serious and are not always easy to detect.

Fortran also lacks various control and data structures which simplify programming in languages with a more modern design. These limitations, and others, should all be eliminated with the advent of Fortran 8x.

1.4 Precautions

Extensions and portability

Computer manufacturers have a natural tendency to compete with each other by providing Fortran systems which are 'better' than before, usually by providing extensions to the language. This does not conflict with the Fortran Standard, provided that standard-conforming programs are still processed correctly. Indeed, in the long term languages advance by the absorption of such extensions. In the short term, however, their use is more problematical, since they necessarily make programs less portable.

When the latest Fortran Standard was issued in 1977 there was fairly widespread disappointment that it did not go just a little further in eliminating some of the tiresome restrictions that had persisted since the early days. The US Department of Defense issued a short list of extensions which manufacturers were encouraged to add to their Fortran 77 systems. The most important of these were the following:

- the END DO statement
- the DO WHILE loop

- the INCLUDE statement
- the IMPLICIT NONE facility
- intrinsic functions for bit-wise logic.

Many Fortran systems, especially those produced in the United States, now support these extensions but they are by no means universal and should not be used in portable programs.

One of the most irksome restrictions of Fortran 77 is that symbolic names cannot be more than six characters long. This forces programmers to devise all manner of contractions, abbreviations, and acronyms in place of meaningful symbolic names. It is very tempting to take advantage of systems which relax this rule but this can have serious repercussions. Consider a program which makes use of variables called TEMPERATURE and TEMPERED. Many compilers will be quite happy with these, though a few will reject both names on grounds of length. Unfortunately there are also one or two compilers in existence which will simply ignore all letters after the sixth so that both names will be taken as references to the same variable, TEMPER. Such behaviour, while deplorable, is quite in accordance with the Standard which only requires systems to compile programs correctly if they conform to its rules.

The only way to be certain of avoiding problems like this is to ignore such temptations entirely and just use Standard Fortran. Many compilers provide a switch or option which can be set to cause all non-standard syntax to be flagged. Everything covered in this book is part of Standard Fortran unless clearly marked to the contrary.

Guidelines

Computer programming always requires a very high standard of care and accuracy if it is to be successful. This is even more vital when using Fortran than with some other languages, because, as explained above, the liberal rules of Fortran make it harder for the system to detect mistakes. To program successfully it is not enough just to conform to the rules of the language, it is also important to defend yourself against known pitfalls.

There is a useful lesson to be learned from the failure of one of the earliest planetary probes launched by NASA. The cause of the failure was eventually traced to a statement in its control software similar to this:

```
DO 15 I = 1.100
```

when what should have been written was:

```
DO 15 I = 1,100
```

but somehow a dot had replaced the comma. Because Fortran ignores spaces, this was seen by the compiler as:

```
DO15I = 1.100
```

which is a perfectly valid assignment to a variable called DO15I and not at all what was intended.

Fortran 77 permits an additional comma to be inserted after the label in a DO statement, so it could now be written as:

```
DO 15,I = 1,100
```

This has the great advantage that it is no longer as vulnerable to a single-point failure.

There are many hazards of this sort in Fortran, but the risk of falling victim to them can be minimised by adopting the programming practices of more experienced users. To help you, various recommendations and guidelines are given throughout this book. Some of the most outdated and unsatisfactory features of Fortran are not described in the main part of the book but have been relegated to Appendix A.

There is not room in a book of this size to go further into the techniques of program design and software engineering. As far as possible everything recommended here is consistent with the methods of modular design and structured programming, but you should study these topics in more detail before embarking on any large-scale programming projects.

2 Basic Fortran Concepts

This chapter presents some of the basic ideas of Fortran by showing some complete examples. In the interests of simplicity, the problems which these solve are hardly beyond the range of a good pocket calculator, and the programs shown here do not include various refinements that would usually be present in professional software. They are, however, complete working programs which you can try out for yourself if you have access to a Fortran system. If not, it is still worth reading through them to see how the basic elements of Fortran can be put together into complete programs.

2.1 Statements

To start with, here is one of the simplest programs that can be devised:

```
PROGRAM TINY
WRITE(UNIT=*, FMT=*) 'Hello, world'
END
```

As you can probably guess, all this program does is to send a rather trite message 'Hello, world' to your terminal. Even so, its layout and structure deserve some explanation.

The program consists of three lines, each containing one *statement*. Each Fortran statement must have a line to itself (or more than one line if necessary), but the first six character positions on each line are reserved for statement labels and continuation markers. Since the statements in this example need neither of these features, the first six columns of each line have been left blank.

The PROGRAM statement gives a name to the program unit and declares that it is a *main program* unit. Other types of program unit will be covered later on. The program can be called anything you like provided the name conforms to the Fortran rules; the first character of a Fortran symbolic name must be a letter but, unfortunately, they cannot be more than six characters long in total. It is generally sensible to give the same name to the program and to the file which holds the Fortran *source code* (the original text).

The WRITE statement produces output: the parentheses enclose a list of *control items* which determine where and in what form the output appears. UNIT=★ selects the standard output file which is normally your own terminal; FMT=★ selects a default output layout (technically known as *list-directed* format). Asterisks are used here, as in many places in Fortran, to select a default or standard option. This program could, in fact, have been made slightly shorter by using an abbreviated form of the WRITE statements:

```
WRITE(*,*) 'Hello, world'
```

Although the keywords UNIT= and FMT= are optional, they help to make the program more readable. The items in the control list, like those in all lists in Fortran, are separated by commas.

The control information in the WRITE statement is followed by a list of the data items to be output: here there is just one item, a character constant which is enclosed in a pair of apostrophe (single quote) characters.

An END statement is required at the end of every program unit. When the program is *compiled* (translated into machine code) it tells the compiler that the program unit is complete; when encountered at run-time the END statement stops the program running and returns control to the operating system.

The Standard Fortran character set does not contain any lower-case letters so statements generally have to be written all in upper case. But Fortran programs can process as *data* any characters supported by the machine; character constants (such as the message in the last example) are not subject to this constraint.

2.2 Expressions and Assignments

The next example solves a somewhat more realistic problem: it computes the repayments on a fixed-term loan (such as a home mortgage loan). The fixed payments cover the interest and repay part of the capital sum; they can be calculated by the following formula:

$$\text{annual repayment} = \frac{\text{rate} \cdot \text{amount}}{(1 - (1+\text{rate})^{-\text{nyears}})}$$

In this formula, *rate* is the annual interest rate expressed as a fraction;

since it is more conventional to quote interest rates as a percentage the program does this conversion for us.

```
PROGRAM LOAN
WRITE(UNIT=*,FMT=*)'Enter amount, %rate, years'
READ(UNIT=*,FMT=*) AMOUNT, PCRATE, NYEARS
RATE = PCRATE / 100.0
REPAY = RATE*AMOUNT/(1.0-(1.0+RATE)**(-NYEARS))
WRITE(UNIT=*,FMT=*)'Annual repayments ',REPAY
END
```

This example introduces two new forms of statement: the READ and *assignment* statements, both of which can be used to assign new values to variables.

The READ statement has a similar form to WRITE: here it reads in three numbers entered on the terminal in response to the prompt and assigns their values to the three named variables. FMT=★ again selects list-directed (or free-format) input which allows the numbers to be given in any convenient form: they can be separated by spaces or commas or even given one on each line.

The fourth statement is an assignment statement which divides PCRATE by 100 and assigns the result to another variable called RATE. The next assignment statement evaluates the loan repayment formula and assigns the result to a variable called REPAY.

Several arithmetic operators are used in these expressions: as in most programming languages, / represents division, and ★ represents multiplication; in Fortran, ★★ is used for exponentiation, i.e. raising one number to the power of another. Note that two operators cannot appear in succession as this could be ambiguous, so that instead of ★★–N the form ★★(–N) has to be used.

Another general point concerning program layout: spaces (blanks) are not significant in Fortran statements so they can be inserted freely to improve the legibility of the program.

When the program is run, the terminal dialogue will look something like this:

```
Enter amount, %rate, years
20000, 9.5, 15
Annual repayments 2554.873
```

The answer given by your system may not be exactly the same as this because the number of digits provided by list-directed formatting depends on the accuracy of the arithmetic, which varies from one computer to another.

2.3 Integer and Real Data Types

The LOAN program would have been more complicated if it had not taken advantage of some implicit rules of Fortran concerning data types: this requires a little more explanation.

Computers can store numbers in several different ways: the most common numerical data types are those called *integer* and *real*. Integer variables store numbers exactly and are mainly used to count discrete objects. Real variables are useful in many other circumstances as they store numbers using a floating-point representation which can handle numbers with a fractional part as well as whole numbers. The disadvantage of the real data type is that floating-point numbers are not stored exactly: typically only the first six or seven decimal digits will be correct. It is important to select the correct type for every data item in the program. In the last example, the number of years was an integer, but all of the other variables were of real type.

The data type of a constant is always evident from its form: character constants, for example, are enclosed in a pair of apostrophes. In numerical constants the presence of a decimal point indicates that they are real and not integer constants: this is why the value one was represented as '1.0' and not just '1'.

There are several ways to specify the data type of a variable. One is to use explicit *type* statements at the beginning of the program. For example, the previous program could have begun like this:

```
PROGRAM LOAN
INTEGER NYEARS
REAL AMOUNT, PCRATE, RATE, REPAY
```
etc.

Although many programming languages require declarations of this sort for every symbolic name used in the program, Fortran does not. Depending on your point of view, this makes Fortran programs easier to write, or allows Fortran programmers to become lazy. The reason that these declarations can often be omitted in Fortran is that, in the absence of an explicit declaration, the data type of any item is determined by the first letter of its name. The general rule is:

    initial letters I–N   *integer type*
    initial letters A–H and O–Z   *real type.*

In the preceding program, because the period of the loan was called NYEARS (and not simply YEARS) it automatically became an integer, while all the other variables were of real type.

2.4 DO-Loops

Although the annual repayments on a home loan are usually fixed, the outstanding balance does not decline linearly with time. The next program demonstrates this with the aid of a DO-loop.

```
         PROGRAM REDUCE
         WRITE(UNIT=*,FMT=*)'Enter amount, %rate, years'
         READ(UNIT=*, FMT=*) AMOUNT, PCRATE, NYEARS
         RATE = PCRATE / 100.0
         REPAY = RATE*AMOUNT/(1.0-(1.0+RATE)**(-NYEARS))
         WRITE(UNIT=*, FMT=*)'Annual repayments', REPAY
         WRITE(UNIT=*, FMT=*)'End of Year  Balance'
         DO 15,IYEAR = 1,NYEARS
             AMOUNT = AMOUNT + (AMOUNT * RATE) - REPAY
             WRITE(UNIT=*, FMT=*) IYEAR, AMOUNT
  15     CONTINUE
         END
```

The first part of the program is similar to the earlier one. It continues with another WRITE statement which produces headings for the two columns of output which will be produced later on.

The DO statement then defines the start of a loop: the statements in the loop are executed repeatedly with the loop-control variable IYEAR taking successive values from 1 to NYEARS. The first statement in the loop updates the value of AMOUNT by adding the annual interest to it and subtracting the actual repayment. This results in AMOUNT storing the amount of the loan still owing at the end of the year. The next statement outputs the year number and the latest value of AMOUNT. After this there is a CONTINUE statement which actually does nothing but act as a place-marker. The loop ends at the CONTINUE statement because it is attached to the label, 15, that was specified in the DO statement at the start of the loop.

The active statements in the loop have been indented a little to the right of those outside them: this is not required but is very common practice among Fortran programmers because it makes the structure of the program more conspicuous.

The program REDUCE produces a table of values which, while mathematically correct, is not very easy to read:

```
Enter amount, % rate, years
2000, 9.5, 5
Annual repayments are 520.8728
End of Year Balance
        1     1669.127
        2     1306.822
        3     910.0968
        4     475.6832
        5     2.9800416E-04
```

2.5 Formatted Output

The table of values would have a better appearance if the decimal points were properly aligned and if there were only two digits after them. The last figure in the table is actually less than a thirtieth of a penny, which is effectively zero to within the accuracy of the machine. A better layout can be produced easily enough by using an explicit *format specification* instead of the list-directed output used up to now. To do this, the last WRITE statement in the program should be replaced with one like this:

```
WRITE(UNIT=*,FMT='(1X,I9,F11.2)')IYEAR, AMOUNT
```

The amended program will then produce a neater tabulation:

```
Enter amount, % rate, years
2000, 9.5, 5
Annual repayments 520.8728
End of Year   Balance
        1     1669.13
        2     1306.82
        3      910.10
        4      475.68
        5         .00
```

The format specification has to be enclosed in parentheses and, as it is actually a character constant, in a pair of apostrophes as well. The first item in the format list, 1X, is needed to cope with the carriage-control convention: it provides an additional blank at the start of each line which is later removed by the Fortran system. There is no logical explanation for this: it is there for compatibility with very early Fortran systems. The remaining items specify the layout of each number: I9 specifies that the first number, an integer, should occupy a field 9 columns wide; similarly, F11.2 puts the second number, a real (floating-point) value, into a field 11 characters wide with exactly 2 digits after the decimal point. Numbers are always right-justified in each field. The field widths in this example have been chosen so that the columns of figures line up satisfactorily with the headings.

2.6 Functions

Fortran provides a useful selection of *intrinsic functions* to carry out various mathematical operations such as square root, maximum and minimum, sine, cosine, etc., as well as various data type conversions. You can also write your own functions. The next example, which computes the area of a triangle, shows both forms of function in action.

The formula for the area of a triangle with sides of length a, b and c is:

area = $[s.(s-a).(s-b).(s-c)]^{0.5}$
where: s = (a + b + c)/2

```
      PROGRAM TRIANG
      WRITE(UNIT=*,FMT=*)'Enter lengths of sides:'
      READ(UNIT=*,FMT=*) SA, SB, SC
      WRITE(UNIT=*,FMT=*)'Area is ', AREA3(SA,SB,SC)
      END

      FUNCTION AREA3(A, B, C)
*Computes the area of a triangle from lengths
*of sides
      S = (A + B + C)/2.0
      AREA3 = SQRT(S * (S-A) * (S-B) * (S-C))
      END
```

This program consists of two program units. The first is the main program, and it has a similar form to those seen earlier. The only novel feature is that the list of items output by the WRITE statement includes a call to a function called AREA3. This computes the area of the triangle. It is an *external function* which is specified by means of a separate program unit technically known as a *function subprogram*.

The external function starts with a FUNCTION statement which names the function and specifies its set of *dummy arguments*. This function has three dummy arguments called A, B and C. The values of the actual arguments, SA, SB and SC, are transferred to the corresponding dummy arguments when the function is called. Variable names used in the external function have no connection with those of the main program: the actual and dummy argument values are connected only by their relative position in each list. Thus SA transfers its value to A, and so on. The name of the function can be used as a variable within the subprogram unit; this variable must be assigned a value before the function returns control, as this is the value returned to the calling program.

Within the function the dummy arguments can also be used as variables. The first assignment statement computes the sum, divides it by two, and assigns it to a local variable, S; the second assignment statement uses the intrinsic function SQRT which computes the square-root of its argument. The result is returned to the calling program by assigning it to the variable which has the same name as the function.

The END statement in a procedure does not cause the program to stop but just returns control to the calling program unit.

There is one other novelty: a comment line describing the action of the function. Any line of text can be inserted as a comment anywhere except after an END statement. Comment lines have an asterisk in the first column.

These two program units could be held on separate source files and even compiled separately. An additional stage, usually called linking, is needed to construct the complete executable program out of these separately compiled object modules. This seems an unnecessary overhead for such simple programs but, as described in the next chapter, it has advantages when building large programs.

In this very simple example it was not really necessary to separate the calculation from the input/output operations but in more complicated cases this is usually a sensible practice. For one thing it allows the same calculation to be executed anywhere else that it is required. For another, it reduces the complexity of the program by dividing the work up into small independent units which are easier to manage.

2.7 IF-Blocks

Another important control structure in Fortran is the IF statement which allows a block of statements to be executed conditionally, or allows a choice to be made between different courses of action.

One obvious defect of the function AREA3 is that it has no protection against incorrect input. Many sets of three real numbers could not possibly form the sides of a triangle, for example 1.0, 2.0, and 7.0. A little analysis shows that in all such impossible cases the argument of the square root function will be negative, which is illegal. Fortran systems should detect errors like this at run-time but will vary in their response. Even so, a message like 'negative argument for square-root' may not be enough to suggest to the user what is wrong. The next version of the function is slightly more user-friendly:

```
      REAL FUNCTION AREA3(A, B, C)
*Computes the area of a triangle from lengths
*of its sides.
*If arguments are invalid issues message and returns
*zero.
      REAL A, B, C
      S = (A + B + C)/2.0
      FACTOR = S * (S-A) * (S-B) * (S-C)
      IF(FACTOR .LE. 0.0) THEN
          WRITE(UNIT=*, FMT=*)'Impossible triangle'
          AREA3 = 0.0
      ELSE
          AREA3 = SQRT(FACTOR)
      END IF
      END
```

The IF statement works with the ELSE and END IF statements to enclose two blocks of code. The statements in the first block are only executed if the expression in the IF statement is *true*, those in the second block only if it is *false*. The statements in each block are indented for visibility, but this is, again, just a sensible programming practice.

With this modification, the value of FACTOR is tested and if it is negative or zero then an error message is produced; AREA3 is also set to an impossible value (zero) to flag the mistake. Note that the form '.LE.' is used because the less-than-or-equals character, '≤', is not present in the Fortran character set. If FACTOR is positive the calculation proceeds as before.

2.8 Arrays

Fortran has good facilities for handling arrays. They can have up to seven dimensions. The program STATS reads a set of real numbers from a data file and puts them into a one-dimensional array. It then computes their mean and standard deviation.

Given an array of values x_1, x_2, x_3, ...x_N, the mean μ and standard deviation σ are given by:

$\mu = \Sigma x_i /N$

$$\sigma^2 = \Sigma(x_i - \mu)^2 / (N-1)$$
$$= (\Sigma x_i^2 - N\mu)/(N-1)$$

To simplify this program, it will be assumed that the first number in the file is an integer which tells the program how many real data points follow.

```
      PROGRAM STATS
      CHARACTER FNAME*50
      REAL X(1000)
      WRITE(UNIT=*, FMT=*) 'Enter data file name:'
      READ(UNIT=*, FMT='(A)') FNAME
      OPEN(UNIT=1, FILE=FNAME, STATUS='OLD')
*Read number of data points NPTS
      READ(UNIT=1, FMT=*) NPTS
      WRITE(UNIT=*, FMT=*) NPTS, ' data points'
      IF(NPTS .GT. 1000) STOP 'Too many data points'
      READ(UNIT=1, FMT=*) (X(I), I = 1,NPTS)
      CALL MEANSD(X, NPTS, AVG, SD)
      WRITE(UNIT=*, FMT=*) 'Mean=', AVG, ' S.D.=',SD
      END

      SUBROUTINE MEANSD(X, NPTS, AVG, SD)
      INTEGER NPTS
      REAL X(NPTS), AVG, SD
      SUM   = 0.0
      SUMSQ = 0.0
      DO 15, I = 1,NPTS
          SUM   = SUM   + X(I)
          SUMSQ = SUMSQ + X(I)**2
15    CONTINUE
      AVG = SUM / NPTS
      SD  = SQRT(SUMSQ - NPTS * AVG)/(NPTS-1)
      END
```

This program has several new statement forms.

The CHARACTER statement declares that the variable FNAME is to hold a string of 50 characters: this should be long enough for the filenames used by most operating systems.

The REAL statement declares an array X with 1000 elements numbered from X(1) to X(1000).

The READ statement uses a format item A which is needed to read in a character string: A originally stood for 'alphanumeric'.

The OPEN statement then assigns I/O unit number one (any small integer could have been used) to the file. This unit number is needed in subsequent input/output statements. STATUS='OLD' indicates that the file already exists.

The IF statement is a special form which can replace an IF-block where it would only contain one statement: its effect is to stop the program running if the array would not be large enough.

The READ statement which follows it has a special form known as an *implied-DO-loop*: this reads all the numbers from the file into successive elements of the array X in one operation.

The CALL statement corresponds to the SUBROUTINE statement in the same way that a function reference corresponded to a FUNCTION statement. The difference is that the arguments X and NPTS transfer information into the subroutine, whereas AVG and SD return information from it. The direction of transfer is determined only by the way the dummy arguments are used within the subroutine. An argument can be used to pass information in either direction, or both.

The INTEGER statement is, as before, not really essential but it is good practice to indicate clearly the data type of every procedure argument.

The REAL statement declares that X is an array but uses a special option available only to dummy arguments: it uses another argument, NPTS, to specify its size and makes it an *adjustable* array. Normally in Fortran, array bounds must be specified by constants, but the rules are relaxed for arrays passed into procedures because the actual storage space is already allocated in the calling program unit; the REAL statement here merely specifies how many of the 1000 elements already allocated are actually to be used within the subroutine.

The rest of the subroutine uses a loop to accumulate the sum of the elements in SUM, and the sum of their squares in SUMSQ. It then computes the mean and standard deviation using the usual formulae, and returns these values to the main program, where they are printed out.

3 Fortran in Practice

This chapter describes the steps required to turn a Fortran program from a piece of text into executable form. The main operation is that of translating the original Fortran *source code* into the appropriate machine code. On a typical Fortran system this is carried out in two separate stages. This chapter explains how this works in more detail.

These descriptions differ from those in the rest of the book in two ways. Firstly, it is not essential to understand how a Fortran system works in order to use it, just as you do not have to know how an internal combustion engine works in order to drive a car. But, in both cases, those who have some basic understanding of the way in which the machine works find it easier to get the best results. This is especially true when things start to go wrong – and most people find that things go wrong all too easily when they start to use a new programming language.

Secondly, the contents of this chapter are much more system-dependent than all the others in the book. The Fortran Standard only specifies what a Fortran program should do when it is executed, it has nothing directly to say about the translation process. In practice, however, nearly all Fortran systems work in much the same way, so there should not be too many differences between the 'typical' system described here and the one that you are actually using. Regrettably, the underlying similarities are sometimes obscured by differences in the terminology that different manufacturers use.

3.1 The Fortran System

The two main ways of translating a program into machine code are to use an *interpreter* or a *compiler*.

An interpreter is a program which stays in control all the while the program is running. It translates the source code into machine code one line at a time and then executes that line immediately. It then goes on to translate the next, and so on. If an error occurs it is usually possible to correct the mistake and continue running the program from the point at which it left off. This can speed up program development considerably. The main snag is that all non-trivial programs involve forms of repetition, such as loops or procedure calls. In all these cases the same lines of source code are translated into machine code over and over again. Some interpreters are clever enough to avoid doing all the work again but the overhead cannot be eliminated entirely.

The compiler works in an entirely different way. It is an independent program which translates the entire source code into machine code at once. The machine code is usually saved on a file, often called an *executable image*, which can then be run whenever it is needed. Because each statement is only translated once, but can be executed as many times as you like, the time taken by the translation process is less important. Many systems provide what is called an *optimising compiler* which takes even more trouble and generates highly efficient machine code; optimised code will try to make the best possible use of fast internal registers and the compiler will analyse the source program in blocks rather than one line at a time. As a result, compiled programs usually run an order of magnitude faster than interpreted ones. The main disadvantage is that if the program fails in any way, it is necessary to edit the source code and recompile the whole thing before starting again from the beginning. The error messages from a compiled program may also be less informative than those from an interpreter because the original symbolic names and line numbers may not be retained by the compiler.

Interpreters, being more 'user-friendly', are especially suitable for highly interactive use and for running small programs produced by beginners. Thus, languages like APL, BASIC, and Logo are usually handled by an interpreter. Fortran, on the other hand, is often used for jobs which consume significant amounts of computer time: in some applications, such as weather forecasting, the results would simply be of no use if they were produced more slowly. The speed advantage of compilers is therefore of great importance and in practice almost all Fortran systems use a compiler to carry out the translation.

Separate compilation

The principal disadvantage of a compiler is the necessity of recompiling the whole program after making any alteration to it, no matter how small. Fortran has partly overcome this limitation by allowing program units to be compiled separately; these compiled units or *modules* are linked together afterwards into an executable program.

A Fortran compiler turns the source code into what is usually called *object code*: this contains the appropriate machine-code instructions but with relative memory addresses rather than absolute ones. All the program units can be compiled together, or each one can be compiled separately. Either way a set of *object modules* is produced, one from each program unit. The second stage, which joins all the object modules together, is usually known as *linking*, but other terms such as *loading*, *link-editing* and *task-building* are also in use. The job of the linker is to collect up all these object modules, allocate absolute addresses to each one, and produce a complete executable program, also called an executable image.

The advantage of this two-stage system is that if changes are made to just one program unit then only that one has to be re-compiled. It is, of course, necessary to re-link the whole program. The operations which the linker performs are relatively simple so that linkers ought to be fast. Unfortunately this is not always so, and on some systems it can take longer to link a small program than to compile it.

3.2 Creating the Source Code

The first step after writing a program is to enter it into the computer: these files are known as the *source code*. Fortran systems do not usually come with an editor of their own: the source files can be generated using any convenient text editor or word processor.

Many text editors have options which ease the drudgery of entering Fortran statements. On some you can define a single key-stroke to skip directly to the start of the statement field at column 7 (but if the source files are to conform to the standard, this should work by inserting a suitable number of spaces and not a *tab* character). An even more useful feature is a warning when you cross the right-margin of the statement field at column 72. Most text editors make it easy to delete and insert whole words, where a *word* is anything delimited by spaces. It helps with later editing, therefore, to put spaces between items in Fortran statements. This also makes the program more readable.

Most programs will consist of several *program units*: these may go on separate files, all on one file, or any combination. On most systems it is not necessary for the main program unit to come first. When first keying in the program it may seem simpler to put the whole program on one file, but during program development it is usually more convenient to have each program unit on a separate file so that they can be edited and compiled independently. It minimises confusion if each source file has the same name as the (first) program unit that it contains.

INCLUDE statements

Many systems provide a pseudo-statement called INCLUDE (or sometimes INSERT) which inserts the entire contents of a separate text file into the source code in place of the INCLUDE statement. This feature can be particularly useful when the same set of statements, usually specification statements, has to be used in several different program units. Such is often the case when defining a set of constants using PARAMETER statements, or when declaring common blocks with a set of COMMON statements. INCLUDE statements reduce the key-punching effort and the risk of error. Although non-standard, INCLUDE statements do not seriously compromise portability because they merely manipulate the source files and do not alter the source code which the compiler translates.

3.3 Compiling

The main function of a Fortran compiler is to read a set of source files and write the corresponding set of object modules to the object file.

Most compilers have a number of switches or options which can be set to control how the compiler works and what additional output it produces. Some of the more useful ones, found on many systems, are described below.

- Almost all compilers can produce a listing file: a text file containing a copy of the source code, with the lines numbered, and with error messages and other useful information attached. A list of all the symbolic names and labels used in the program unit is often provided: this should be checked for unexpected entries as they may be the result of spelling mistakes.

- An even more useful addition to the listing is a cross-reference table: this lists every place that each symbolic name has been used. Good compilers indicate which names have only been used once as these often indicate a programming mistake.

- Another widely available option is the detection of syntax which does not conform to the Fortran Standard: this helps to ensure program portability.

- Often it is possible to choose the optimisation level. During program development a low level of optimisation should be selected if this makes the *compiler* run faster; it may improve the error detection. Highly optimised machine code may execute faster but if the source code lines are rearranged error messages may be less helpful.

- Many systems allow additional code to be included which check for errors at run-time. Errors such as over-running the bounds of an array or a character string, or arithmetic overflow can usually be trapped. Such errors are not uncommon, so this assistance is very valuable. Some programming manuals suggest that these options should only be selected during program development and switched off thereafter in the interests of speed. This is rather like wearing seat-belts in the car only while you are learning to drive and ignoring them as soon as you are allowed out on the motorway. Run-time checks do not usually reduce the execution speed noticeably.

3.4 Linking

At its simplest, the linker just takes the set of object modules produced by the compiler and links them all together into an executable image. One of these modules must correspond to the main program unit; the other modules will correspond to procedures and to block data subprogram units.

It often happens that a number of different programs require some of the same computations to be carried out. If these calculations can be turned into procedures and linked into each program it can save a great deal of programming effort, especially in the long run. This 'building block' approach is particularly beneficial for large programs. Many organisations gradually build up collections of procedures which become an important software resource. Procedures collected in this way tend to be fairly reliable and free from bugs, if only because they have been extensively tested and debugged in earlier applications.

Object libraries

It obviously saves on compilation time if these commonly-used procedures can be kept in compiled form as object modules. Almost all operating systems allow a collection of object modules to be stored in an *object library* (sometimes known as a pre-compiled or relocatable-code library). This is a file containing a collection of object modules together with an index which allows them to be extracted easily. Object libraries are not only more efficient but also easier to use as there is only one file-name to specify to the linker. The linker can then work out for itself which modules are needed to satisfy the various CALL statements and function references encountered in the preceding object modules. Object libraries also simplify the management of a procedure collection and may reduce the amount of disc space needed. There are usually simple ways of listing the contents of an object library, deleting modules from it, and replacing modules with new versions.

All Fortran systems come with a *system library* which contains the object modules for various intrinsic functions such as SIN, COS and SQRT. This is automatically scanned by the linker and does not have to be specified explicitly.

Software is often available commercially in the form of procedure libraries containing modules which may be linked into any Fortran program. Those commonly used cover fields such as statistics, signal processing, graphics, and numerical analysis.

Linker options

The order of the object modules supplied to the linker does not usually matter, although some systems require the main program to be specified first. The order in which the library files are searched may be important, however, so that some care has to be exercised when several different libraries are in use at the same time.

The principal output of the linker is a single file usually called the executable image. Most linkers can also produce a storage map showing the location of the various modules in memory. Sometimes other information is provided such as symbol tables which may be useful in debugging the program.

3.5 Program Development

The program development process consists of a number of stages some of which may have to be repeated several times until the end product is correct:

(1) Designing the program and writing the source-code text.
(2) Keying in the text to produce a set of Fortran source files.
(3) Compiling the source code to produce a set of object modules.
(4) Linking the object modules and any object libraries into a complete executable image.

(5) Running the executable program on some test data and checking the results

The main parts of the process are shown below diagrammatically.

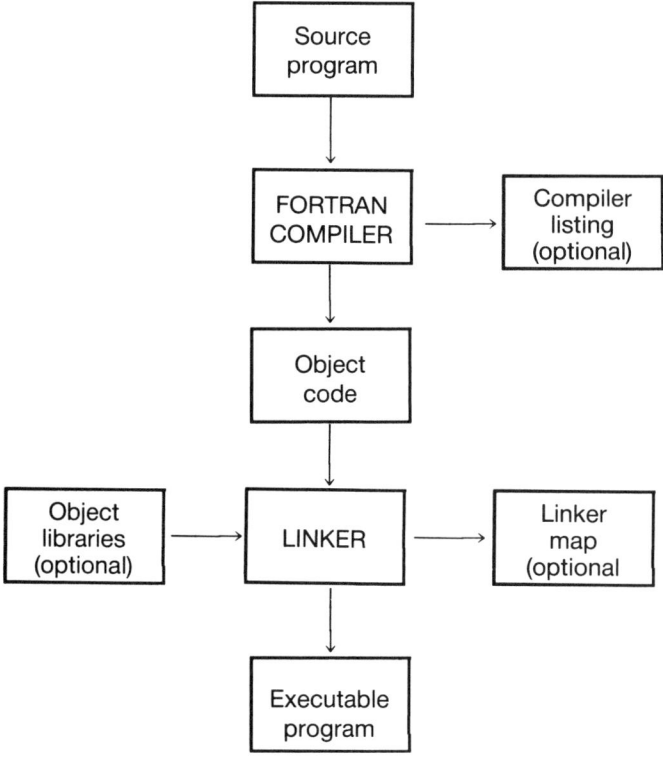

Handling errors

Things can go wrong at almost every stage of the program development process for a variety of reasons, most of them the fault of the programmer. Naturally, the Fortran system cannot possibly detect all the mistakes that it is possible for human programmers to make. Errors in the syntax of Fortran statements can usually be detected by the compiler, which will issue error messages indicating what is wrong and, if possible, where.

Other mistakes will only come to light at the linking stage. If, for example, you misspell the name of a subroutine or function, the compiler will not be able to detect this as it only works on one program unit at a time, but the linker will say something like 'unsatisfied external reference'. This sort of message will sometimes appear if you misspell the name of an array since array and function references can have the same form.

Most errors that occur at run-time are the result of programmer error, or at least failure to anticipate some failure mode. Even things like division by zero or attempting to access an array element which is beyond its declared bounds can be prevented by sufficiently careful programming.

There is, however, a second category of run-time error which no amount of forethought can avoid: these nearly all involve the input/output system. Examples include trying to open a file which no longer exists, or finding corrupted data on an input file. For this reason most input/output errors can be trapped, using the IOSTAT= or ERR= keywords in any I/O statement. There is no way of trapping run-time errors in any other types of statement in Standard Fortran.

But, just because a program compiles, links and runs without apparent error, it is not safe to assume that all bugs have been eliminated. There are some types of mistake which will simply give you the wrong answer. The only way to become confident that a program is correct is to give it some test data, preferably for a case where the results can be calculated independently. When a program is too elaborate for its results to be predictable it should be split into sections which can be checked separately.

4 Program Structure and Layout

This chapter explains the rules for program construction and text layout. A complete Fortran program is composed of a number of separate *program units*. Each of these can contain both *statements* and *comment lines*. Statements are formed from items such as *keywords* and *symbolic names*. These in turn consist of characters.

4.1 The Fortran Character Set

The only characters needed to write Fortran programs, and the only ones that should be used in portable software, are those in the Fortran character set:

the 26 upper-case letters   A B C ... X Y Z
the 10 digits   0 1 2 3 4 5 6 7 8 9
and 13 special characters:

+	plus	−	minus
*	asterisk	/	slash
	blank	=	equals
(	left parenthesis	)	right parenthesis
.	decimal point	,	comma
'	apostrophe	:	colon
$	currency symbol		

Although this character set is somewhat limited, it is at least universally available, which helps to make programs portable. What suffers is program legibility: lower-case letters are absent and it is necessary to resort to ugly constructions like .LT. and .GT. to represent operators like < and >. Some of the special characters, such as the asterisk and parentheses, are also rather overloaded with duties.

Blanks

The blank, or space, character is ignored everywhere in Fortran statements (except within *character constants*, which are enclosed in a pair of apostrophes). Although you do not need to separate items in Fortran statements with blanks, it is good practice to include a liberal helping of them since they improve legibility and often simplify editing. The only limitation (as explained below) is that statement lines must not extend beyond column 72.

Currency symbol

The currency symbol has no fixed graphic representation: it appears on most systems as the dollar ($), but systems which use other forms such as £ or ¥ are equally valid. This variability does not matter much because the currency symbol is not actually needed in Standard Fortran syntax.

Other characters

Most computers have a character set which includes many other printable characters, for example lower-case letters, square brackets, ampersands and per-cent signs. Any printable characters supported by the machine may be used in *comment lines* and within *character constants*.

The Fortran character set does not include any carriage-control characters such as *tab*, *carriage-return* or *form-feed*, but formatted WRITE statements can be used to produce paginated and tabulated output files.

Fortran programs can process as *data* any characters supported by the local hardware. The Fortran Standard is not based on the use of any particular character code but it requires its character comparison functions to use the collating sequence of the American Standard Code for Information Interchange (ASCII). Further details are given in section 7.6.

4.2 Statements and Lines

The statement is the smallest unit of a Fortran program, corresponding to what is called an instruction or command in some programming languages. Most types of statement start with a *keyword* which consists of one (or sometimes two) English words describing the main action of that statement, for example: READ, DO, ELSE IF, GO TO. Since blanks are ignored, compound keywords can be written either as one word or two: ELSEIF or ELSE IF (but the latter seems easier to read).

The rules for statement layout are an unfortunate relic of punched-card days. Every statement must start on a new line and each line is divided into three fixed fields:

(1) columns 1 to 5 form the *label* field,
(2) column 6 forms the *continuation marker* field,
(3) columns 7 to 72 form the *statement* field.

Since labels and continuation markers are only needed on a few statements, the first six columns of most lines are left blank.

Any characters in column 73 or beyond are likely to be ignored (columns 73 to 80 were once used to hold card sequence numbers). This invisible boundary after column 72 demands careful attention as it can have very pernicious effects: it is possible for a statement to be truncated at the boundary but still be syntactically correct, so that the compiler will not detect anything wrong.

Continuation lines

Statements do not have to fit on a single line. The initial line of each statement should have a blank in column 6, and all subsequent lines, called continuation lines, must have some character other than blank or the digit zero in column 6. Up to 19 continuation lines are allowed, i.e. 20 in total. The column layout needed with continuation lines is illustrated here:

```
columns
123456789...
      IF(REPLY .EQ. 'Y' .OR. REPLY .EQ. 'y' .OR.
     $    REPLY .EQ. 'T' .OR. REPLY .EQ. 't') THEN
```

The currency symbol makes a good continuation marker since if accidentally misplaced into an adjacent column it would be almost certain to produce an error during compilation.

The END statement is an exception to the continuation rule: it may not be followed by continuation lines and no other statement may have an initial line which just contains the letters 'END'. Neither rule causes many problems in practice.

Programs which make excessive use of continuation lines can be hard to read and to modify: it is generally better, if possible, to divide a long statement into several shorter ones.

Comment lines

Comments form an important part of any computer program even though they are completely ignored by the compiler: their purpose is to help any human who has to read and understand the program (such as the original programmer six months later).

Comments in Fortran always occupy a separate line of text; they are marked by an asterisk in the first column. For example:

```
*Calculate the atmospheric refraction at PRESS mbar.
      REF = PRESS *(0.1594 + 1.96E-2 * A + 2E-5 * A**2)
*Correct for the temperature T (Celsius)
      TCOR = (273.0+T)*(1.0 + 0.505*A + 8.45E-2 * A**2)
```

A comment may appear at any point in a program unit except after the END statement (unless another program unit follows, in which case it will form the first line of the next unit). A completely blank line is also allowed and is treated as a blank comment. This means that a blank line is not actually permitted after the last END statement of a program.

There is no limit to the number of consecutive comment lines which may be used; comments may also appear in the middle of a sequence of continuation lines. To conform to the Fortran Standard, comment lines should not be over 72 characters long, but this rule is rarely enforced.

Comments may include characters which are not in the Fortran character set. It helps to distinguish comments from code if they are mainly written in lower-case letters (where available). It is also good practice for comments to precede the statements they describe rather than follow them.

Some systems allow end-of-line comments, usually prefaced by an exclamation mark: this is not permitted by the Fortran standard. For compatibility with Fortran 66 comments can also be denoted by the letter C in column 1.

Statement labels

A label can be attached to any statement. There are three reasons for using labels:

- the end of each DO-loop is specified by a label given in the DO statement;
- every FORMAT statement must have a label attached as that is how READ and WRITE statements refer to it;
- any executable statement may have a label attached so that control may be transferred to it, for example by a GO TO statement.

Example:

```
*Read numbers from input file until it ends, add them
*up.
      SUM = 0.0
100   READ(UNIT=IN, FMT=200, END=9999) VALUE
200   FORMAT(F20.0)
      SUM = SUM + VALUE
      GO TO 100
9999  WRITE(UNIT=*, FMT=*)'SUM of values is', SUM
```

Each label has the form of an unsigned integer in the range 1 to 99999. Blanks and leading zeros are ignored. The numerical value is irrelevant and cannot be used in a calculation at all. The label must appear in columns 1 to 5 of the initial line of the statement. In continuation lines the label field must be blank.

A label must be unique within a program unit, but labels in different program units are quite independent. Although any statement may be labelled, it only makes sense to attach a label to a FORMAT statement or an executable statement, since there is no way of using a label on any other type of statement.

Statement labels are unsatisfactory because nearly all of them mark a point to which control could be transferred from elsewhere in the program unit. This makes it much harder to understand a program with many labelled statements. Unfortunately at present one cannot avoid using labels altogether in Fortran. If labels are used at all they should appear in ascending order and preferably in steps of 10 or 100 to allow for changes. Labels do not have to be right-justified in the label field.

4.3 Program Units

A complete executable program consists of one or more program units. There is always one (and only one) *main program* unit: this starts with a PROGRAM statement. There may also be any number of *subprogram* units of any of the three varieties:

- *subroutine* subprograms: these start with a SUBROUTINE statement
- *function* subprograms, also known as *external functions*: these start with a FUNCTION statement
- *block data* subprograms: these start with a BLOCK DATA statement.

Subroutines and external functions are known collectively as *external procedures*; block data subprograms are not procedures and are used only for the special purpose of initialising the contents of named common blocks.

Every program unit must end with an END statement.

Procedures

Subroutines and external functions are collectively known as *external procedures*: they are described in full in Chapter 9. A *procedure* is a self-contained sequence of operations which can be called into action on demand from elsewhere in the program. Fortran supplies a number of intrinsic functions such as SIN, COS, TAN, MIN, MAX, etc. These are procedures which are automatically available when you need to use them in expressions. External functions can be used in similar ways: there may be any number of arguments but only one value is returned via the function name.

The subroutine is a procedure of more general form: it can have any number of input and output arguments but it is executed only in response to an explicit CALL statement.

Procedures may call other procedures and so on, but a procedure may not call itself directly or indirectly: Fortran does not support recursive procedure calls.

Most Fortran systems allow procedures to be written in other languages and linked with Fortran modules into an executable program. If the procedure interface is similar to that of a Fortran subroutine or function this presents no problem.

The normal way to transfer information from one program unit to another is to use the *argument list* of the procedure as described in Chapter 9, but it is also possible to use a *common block*: a shared area of memory. This facility, which is less modular, is described in Chapter 12.

4.4 Statement Types and Order

Fortran statements are either *executable* or *non-executable*. The compiler translates executable statements directly into a set of machine code instructions. Non-executable statements are mainly used to tell the compiler about the program; they are not directly translated into machine code. The END statement is executable and so are all those in the lowest right-hand box of Table 4.1 below; all other statements are non-executable.

The general order of statements in a program unit is:

(1) Program unit header (PROGRAM, SUBROUTINE, FUNCTION or BLOCK DATA statement)
(2) Specification statements
(3) Executable statements
(4) END statement.

Table 4.1 shows shows the complete statement ordering rules: the statements listed in each box can be intermixed with those in boxes on the same horizontal level (thus PARAMETER statements can be intermixed with IMPLICIT statements) but those in boxes separated vertically must appear in the proper order in each program unit (thus all *statement functions* must precede all executable statements).

Table 4.1 Statement ordering rules

	PROGRAM, FUNCTION, SUBROUTINE, BLOCK DATA	
FORMAT	PARAMETER	IMPLICIT

		Type statements:
		   INTEGER, REAL, DOUBLE PRECISION,
		   COMPLEX, LOGICAL, CHARACTER
		Other specification statements:
		   COMMON, DIMENSION, EQUIVALENCE,
		   EXTERNAL, INTRINSIC, SAVE

	DATA	Statement function statements

		Executable statements:
		   BACKSPACE, CALL, CLOSE, CONTINUE, DO,
		   ELSE, ELSE IF, END IF, GO TO, IF,
		   INQUIRE, OPEN, READ, RETURN, REWIND,
		   STOP, WRITE, *assignment* statements

	END	

Execution sequence

A program starts by executing the first executable statement of the main program unit. Execution continues sequentially unless control is transferred elsewhere: an IF or GO TO statement, for example, may transfer control to another part of the same program unit, whereas a CALL statement or function reference will transfer control temporarily to a procedure.

A program continues executing until it reaches a STOP statement in any program unit, or the END statement of the main program unit, or until a fatal error occurs. When a program terminates normally (at STOP or END) the Fortran system closes any files still open before returning control to the operating system. But when a program is terminated prematurely, files, especially output files, may be left with incomplete or corrupted records.

4.5 Symbolic Names

Symbolic names can be given to items such as variables, arrays, constants, functions, subroutines and common blocks. All symbolic names must conform to the following simple rule: the first character of each name must be a letter, this may be followed by up to five more letters or digits. Here are some examples of valid symbolic names:

```
I          MATRIX    VOLTS    PIBY4
OLDCHI     TWOX      R2D2     OUTPUT
```

And here are some names which do not conform to the rules:

```
COMPLEX    (too many letters)
MAX_EL     (underscore is not allowed)
2PI        (starts with a digit)
Height     (lower-case letters are not allowed).
```

It is best to avoid using digits in names unless the meaning is clear, because they are often misread. The digit 1 is easily confused with the letter I, similarly 0 looks much like the letter O on many devices.

The six-character limit on the length of a symbolic name is one of the most unsatisfactory features of Fortran: programs are much harder to understand if the names are cryptic acronyms or abbreviations, but with only six characters there is little choice. Although many systems do not enforce the limit (and the proposal for Fortran 8x is to allow names up to 32 characters long), at present the only way to ensure software portability is to keep strictly to it.

There is a further problem with items which have an associated *data type* (constants, variables, arrays and functions). Unless the data type is declared explicitly in a *type* statement, it is determined by the initial letter of the name. This may further restrict the choice.

Scope of symbolic names

Symbolic names which identify common blocks and program units of all types are *global* in scope, i.e. their name must be unique in the entire executable program. Names identifying all other items (variables, arrays, constants, statement functions, intrinsic functions, and all types of dummy argument) are *local* to the program unit in which they are used so that the same name may be used independently in other program units.

To see the effect of these rules here is a simple example. Suppose your program contains a subroutine called SUMMIT. This is a *global* name so it cannot be used as the name of a global item (such as an external procedure or a common block) in the same executable program. In the SUMMIT subroutine and in any other program unit which calls it, the name cannot be used for a local item such as a variable or array. In all other program units, however, including those which call SUMMIT indirectly, the name SUMMIT can be used freely e.g. for a constant, variable, or array.

The names of global items need to be chosen more carefully because it is harder to alter them at a later stage; it can be difficult to avoid name clashes when writing a large program or building a library of procedures unless program unit names are allocated systematically. It seems appropriate for procedures to have names which are verb-like. If you find it difficult to devise sensible procedure names remember that the English language is well stocked with three and four-letter verbs which form a good basis, for example: DO, ASK, GET, PUT, TRY, EDIT, FORM, LIST, LOAD, SAVE, PLOT. By combining a word like one of these with one or two additional letters it is possible to make up a whole range of procedure names.

Reserved words

In most computer languages there is a long list of words which are reserved by the system and cannot be used as symbolic names: Cobol programmers, for example, have to try to remember nearly 500 of them.

In Fortran there are no reserved words. Some Fortran keywords (for instance DATA, END and OPEN) are short enough to be perfectly valid symbolic names. Although it is not against the rules to do this, it can be somewhat confusing.

The names of the intrinsic functions (such as SQRT, MIN, CHAR) are, technically, *local* names and there is nothing to prevent you using them for your own purposes, but this is not generally a good idea either. For example, if you choose to use the name SQRT for a local variable you will have more difficulty in computing square-roots in that program unit. It is even more unwise to use the name of an intrinsic function as that of an external procedure because in this case the name has to be declared in an EXTERNAL statement in every program unit in which it is used in this way.

4.6 PROGRAM Statement

The PROGRAM statement can only appear at the start of the main program unit. Its only function is to indicate what type of program unit it is and to give it a symbolic name. Although this name cannot be used anywhere else in the program, it may be used by the Fortran system to identify error messages etc. The general form is simply:

> PROGRAM *name*

where *name* is a symbolic name. This name is global in scope and may not be used elsewhere in the main program or as a global name in any other program unit. For compatibility with Fortran 66 the PROGRAM statement is optional. This can have unexpected effects: if you forget to use a SUBROUTINE or FUNCTION statement at the start of a procedure the compiler will assume it to be a (nameless) main program unit. Since this will normally result in two main program units, the linker is likely to detect the mistake.

4.7 END Statement

The END statement must appear as the last statement of every program unit. It simply consists of the word

> END

which may not be followed by any continuation lines (or comments). The END statement is *executable* and may have a label attached. If an

END statement is executed in a subprogram unit, i.e. a procedure, it returns control to the calling unit; if an END statement is executed in the main program it closes any files which are open, stops the program, and returns control to the operating system.

5 Constants, Variables and Arrays

This chapter deals with the data-storage elements of Fortran: constants, variables and arrays. These all possess an important property called *data type*. The data type of an item determines what sort of information it holds and the operations that can be performed on it.

5.1 Data Types

All the information processed by a digital computer is held internally in the form of binary digits or *bits*. Suitable collections of bits can be used to represent many different types of data including numbers and strings of characters. It is not necessary to know how the information is represented internally in order to write Fortran programs, only that there is a different representation for each type of data. The *data type* of each item also determines what operations can be carried out on it: thus, arithmetic operations can be carried out on numbers, whereas character strings can be split up or joined together. The data type of each item is fixed when the program is written.

Fortran, with its emphasis on numerical operations, has four data types just for numbers. These are collectively known as the *arithmetic data types*. Arithmetic expressions can include mixtures of data types and, in most cases, automatic type conversions are provided. In other circumstances, however, especially in procedure calls, there is no provision for automatic type conversion and it is essential for data types to match exactly.

The range and precision of the arithmetic data types are not specified by the Standard: typical values are indicated below, but the only way to be sure is to check the manuals provided with your own Fortran system.

Several intrinsic functions are available to convert from one data type to another. Conversion from character strings to numbers and vice versa can be complicated; these are best carried out with the internal file READ and WRITE statements (see section 10.3).

There are, as yet, no user-defined or structured data types in Fortran.

Standard data types

Table 5.1 summarises the properties of the six data types provided in Standard Fortran:

Table 5.1 Standard data types

Data type	Characteristics
Integer	Whole numbers stored exactly.
Real	Numbers, which may have fractional parts, stored using a floating-point represenatation with limited precision.
Double precision	Similar to *real* but with greater precision.
Complex	Complex numbers: stored as an ordered pair of *real*.
Logical	A Boolean value, i.e. one which is either *true* or *false*.
Character	A string of characters of fixed length.

The first four types (integer, real, double precision and complex) all hold numerical information and are collectively known as *arithmetic data types*.

Integer type

The integer data type can only represent whole numbers but they are stored exactly in all circumstances. Integers are often used to count discrete objects such as elements of an array, characters in a string, or iterations of a loop.

The range of numbers covered by the integer type is system-dependent. The majority of computers use 32 bits for their integer arithmetic (1 bit for the sign and 31 for the magnitude) giving a number range of −2,147,483,648 to +2,147,483,647. Some systems have an even larger integer range but a few very small systems only allow 16-bit integer arithmetic so that their integer range is only −32,768 to +32,767.

Real Type

Most scientific applications use the *real* data type more than anything else. Real values are stored internally using a floating-point representation which gives a larger range than the integer type but the values are not, in general, stored exactly. Both the range and precision are machine-dependent.

In practice most machines use at least 32 bits to store real numbers. Many systems now use the IEEE Standard representation: for 32-bit numbers this gives a precision of just over 7 decimal digits and allows a number range from around 10^{-38} to just over 10^{+38}. This can be something of a limitation because there are many types of calculation, especially in physics and astronomy, which lead to numbers in excess of 10^{40}. Some computers designed expressly for scientific work, sometimes called 'supercomputers', allocate 60 or even 64 bits for real numbers so that the numerical precision is much greater; the range is often larger as well. On such machines it is rarely necessary to use the *double precision* type.

Double precision type

Double precision is an alternative floating-point type. The Fortran Standard only specifies that it should have greater precision than the *real* type but in practice, since the double precision storage unit is twice the size, it is safe to assume that the precision is at least doubled. The number range may, however, be the same as that for real type.

Although double precision values occupy twice as much memory as real (or integer) values, computations on them do not necessarily take twice as long.

Complex type

The *complex* data type stores two *real* values as a single entity. There is no double precision complex type in Standard Fortran.

Complex numbers arise naturally when extracting the roots of negative numbers and are used in many branches of mathematics, physics and engineering. A complex number is often represented as $(A + iB)$, where A and B are the *real* and *imaginary* parts respectively and $i^2 = -1$. Electrical engineers, having used the letter i to represent current, use the notation $(A + jB)$ instead.

Although the rules for manipulating complex numbers are straightforward, it is convenient to have the Fortran system do the work. It is usually more efficient as well, because the computer can use its internal registers to store the intermediate products in complex arithmetic. Exponentiation and the four regular arithmetic operators can be used on complex values, and various intrinsic functions are also provided such as square-root, logarithms and the trigonometric functions.

Logical type

The *logical* data type is mainly used in conjunction with IF statements which select a course of action according to whether some condition is *true* or *false*. A logical variable (or array element) may be used to store such a condition value for future use. Logical variables and arrays are also useful when dealing with two-valued data such as whether a person is male or female, a file open or closed, power on or off, etc.

Some programmers seem reluctant to use logical variables and arrays because they feel that it must be inefficient to use an entire computer word of perhaps 32 bits to store just one bit of information. In fact the extra code needed to implement a more efficient data packing scheme usually wastes more memory than the logical variables would have occupied.

Character type

The *character* type is unique in that each character item has a *length* defined for it: this is the number of characters that it holds. In general the length is fixed when the item is declared and cannot be altered during execution. The only exception to this is for dummy arguments of procedures: here it is possible for the dummy argument to acquire the length of the corresponding actual argument. Using this facility, general-purpose procedures can be written to operate on character strings irrespective of their length. In addition, the rules for character assignment take care of mismatched lengths by truncating or padding with blanks on the right as necessary. This means that the Fortran character type has many of the properties of a genuine variable-length character-handling system.

The maximum length of a character item is system-dependent: it is safe to assume that all systems will allow strings of up to 255 characters, a length limit of 32,767 (or even more) is quite common. The minimum length of a character item is one character; empty or null strings are not permitted.

Storage units

Although the Fortran Standard does not specify the absolute amount of memory to be allocated to each data type, it does specify the relative amounts. This is not important very often, only when constructing unformatted direct-access records or when using COMMON and EQUIVALENCE statements. The rules are as follows:

Table 5.2 Storage units

Data Type	Storage units
Integer, real, logical	1 numerical storage unit
Complex, double precision	2 numerical storage units
character*(N)	N character storage units

In the case of an array the number of storage units must be multiplied by the total number of elements in the array.

The relationship between the numeric and character storage units is deliberately undefined because it is entirely system-dependent.

Guidelines

It is usually fairly clear which data type to choose for each item in a program, though there are some borderline cases among the various arithmetic data types.

When processing data which are inherently integers, such as the number of seeds which germinate in each plot, or the number of photons detected in each time interval, it is not always clear whether to use integer or real arrays to store them. They use the same memory space but on some machines additions and subtractions are faster on integers than on floating-point numbers. In practice, however, any savings can be swallowed up in the data type conversions that are usually necessary in subsequent processing. The main snag with integers is the limited range; on some machines integer overflow is not detected whereas floating-point overflows nearly always produce error messages.

If your machine stores its real variables in 32-bit words then the precision of around 1 in 10^7 is likely to be inadequate in some applications. This imprecision is equivalent to an error of several pence in a million pounds, or around ten milliseconds in a day. If errors of this order are significant you should consider using the double precision type instead. This will normally reduce the errors by at least another factor of 10^7. Mixing data types increases the risks of making mistakes and it is often simpler and safer to use the double precision type instead of real throughout the program, even though this may use slightly more memory and processor time.

Although automatic type conversions are provided for the arithmetic types in expressions, in other cases such as procedure calls it is essential for each actual argument to have the same data type as the corresponding dummy argument. Since program units are compiled independently, it is difficult for either the compiler or the linker to detect type mismatches in calls to external procedures.

Non-standard data types

Although Standard Fortran only provides the above six data types, many systems provide additional ones.

You may come across data type names such as: LOGICAL★1, INTEGER★2, REAL★8, COMPLEX★16, etc. The number after the asterisk indicates the number of bytes of storage used for each datum (a *byte* being a group of 8 bits). This notation has a certain logic but is totally non-standard. The use of a term like REAL★8 when it is simply a synonym for DOUBLE PRECISION seems particularly pointless. There are, of course, circumstances when types such as COMPLEX★16 are necessary but the price to be paid is the loss of portability.

5.2 Constants

A constant has a value which is fixed when the program is written. The data type of every constant is evident from its form. Arithmetic constants always use the decimal number base: Standard Fortran does not support other number bases such as octal or hexadecimal.

Although arithmetic constants may in general have a leading sign (plus or minus) there are some circumstances in Fortran when an *unsigned* constant is required. If the constant is zero then any sign is ignored.

Integer constants

The general form of an integer constant is a sign (plus or minus) followed by a string of one or more digits. All other characters (except blanks) are prohibited. If the number is positive the plus sign is optional. Here are some examples of valid integer constants:

$$-100 \qquad 42$$
$$0 \qquad +1048576$$

It is easier to read a large number if its digits are marked off in groups of three: traditionally the comma (or in some countries the dot) is used for this purpose. The blank can be used in the same way in Fortran programs (but not in data files):

$$-1\ 000\ 000\ 000$$

Note that this number, although conforming to the rules of Fortran, may be too large in magnitude to be stored as an integer on some systems.

Real constants

A real constant must contain a decimal point or an exponent (or both) to distinguish it from one of integer type. The letter 'E' is used in Fortran to represent 'times 10 to the power of'. For example, the constant 1.234×10^{-5} is written as '1.234E−5'.

The most general form of a real constant is:

```
sign    digits        .  digits      E  sign    digits
      ◀integer-part▶    ◀decimal-part▶        ◀exponent▶
◀─────────basic  real  constant─────▶◀─exponent section─▶
```

Both signs are optional; a plus sign is assumed if no sign is present. Leading zeros in the integer-part and in the exponent are ignored. Either the integer part or the decimal part may be omitted if it is zero, but one or the other must be present. If the value of the exponent is zero the entire exponent section may be omitted provided a decimal point is present in the number.

There is no harm in giving more decimal digits in a real (or double precision) constant than the computer can make use of: the value will be correctly rounded by the computer and the extra decimal places ignored.

Here are a few examples of valid real constants:

$$.5 \quad -10. \quad 1E3 \quad P+123.456E4 \quad .000001$$

Dangling decimal points, though permitted, are easily overlooked, and it is conventional to standardise constants in exponential notation so that there is only one digit before the decimal point. Using this convention, these values would look like this:

    0.5   -10.0   1.0E3   1.23456E6   1.0E-6

Double precision constants

A *double precision* constant has a similar form to a *real* constant but it must contain an exponent using the letter 'D' in place of 'E' even if the exponent is zero. Some examples of double precision constants are:

    3.14159265358987D0
    1.0D-12
    -3.652564D+02

Complex constants

A complex constant has the form of two *real* or *integer* constants separated by a comma and enclosed in a pair of parentheses. The first number is the real component and the second the imaginary component. Some examples of valid complex constants are:

    (3.14,-5.67)
    (+1E5,0.125)
    (0,0)
    (-0.999,2.718E15)

Logical constants

There are only two possible logical constants, and they are expressed as:

    .TRUE.
    .FALSE.

The dots at each end are needed to distinguish these special forms from the words TRUE and FALSE, which could be used as symbolic names.

Character constants

A character constant consists of a string of characters enclosed in a pair of apostrophes which act as quotation marks. Within the quoted string any characters available in the character set of the machine are permitted; the blank (or space) character is significant within character constants and counts as a single character just like any other. Examples of valid character constants are:

```
'X'
' £40 + 15%'
'This is a constant including spaces'
```

The apostrophe character can be included in a character constant by representing it as two successive apostrophes (with no intervening blanks). This pair of apostrophes only counts as a single character for the purposes of computing the length of the string. For example:

```
'DON''T'
```

is a constant of length 5.

5.3 Specifying Data Type

The preceding rules ensure that the data type of a literal constant is completely determined by its form. Similarly the data type of an expression depends on the operands and operators involved. The intrinsic functions are also a special case, since their properties, including their data types, are known to the compiler. All other typed objects in a Fortran program are referred to by symbolic names. The rules given here apply to all of these named objects: variables, arrays, named constants, statement functions and external functions.

In many programming languages, especially those in the Algol family, the data type of almost every item in the program has to be specified explicitly. Many programmers regard it as a chore to have to provide all these type specifications, although their presence does make it rather easier for the compiler to detect mistakes.

In Fortran you can specify data types explicitly in a similar way by using *type statements*, but Fortran also makes life easier by having certain default types. The data type of any object which has not been declared in a type statement depends on the first letter of its name. The default rules are:

First letter of the name	Implicit type
I to N	INTEGER
A to H or O to Z	REAL

Most programs make extensive use of integer and real objects, so these default values reduce the number of type statements that are required, provided suitable initial letters are chosen for the symbolic names.

The first-letter rule can also be changed throughout a program unit by using an IMPLICIT statement, described below.

Type statements

There are six different type statements, one for each data type. In their simplest form they just consist of the appropriate data-type keyword followed by a list of symbolic names. For example:

```
INTEGER AGE, GRADE
LOGICAL SUPER
REAL RATE, HOURS, PAY, TAX, INSURE
```

In this example the first four items declared to be *real* would have had that type anyway had the default rules been left to operate. Confirmatory type specification does no harm.

There is no limit to the number of type statements that can be used but a name must not have its type specified explicitly more than once in a program unit. Type statements must precede all executable statements in the unit; it is good practice, though not essential, for them to precede other specification statements referring to the same name. Type statements can be used in a subprogram to specify the types of the dummy arguments and, in an external function, the type of the function as well. Type statements by themselves have no effect on intrinsic function names.

The CHARACTER statement is slightly different from the others because it also specifies the *length* of each character item, i.e. the number of characters it holds. The length can be given separately for each item, thus:

```
CHARACTER NAME*15, STREET*30, TOWN*20, PCODE*7
```

Alternatively, if several items are to have the same length, a default length for the statement can be given at the beginning:

```
CHARACTER*20 STAR, GALAXY, COMET*4, PLANET
```

This declares the name COMET to have a length of 4 characters, whereas STAR, GALAXY and PLANET are all 20 characters long. If the length is not specified at all it defaults to one. The length can also be specified by means of a named integer constant or an *integer constant expression* enclosed in parentheses. For example:

```
PARAMETER (NEXT=15, LAST=80)
CHARACTER TEXT*(NEXT+LAST)
```

Note that the length of a character item is fixed at compilation time. The special form:

```
CHARACTER NAME*(*)
```

is permitted in two cases: for named constants the length of the literal constant in the PARAMETER statement is used (section 5.4); for dummy arguments of procedures the length of the associated actual argument is used (section 9.5). Type statements can also be used to declare the dimensions of arrays: this is described in section 5.6.

IMPLICIT statement

The IMPLICIT statement can be used to change the first-letter default rule throughout a program unit. For example:

```
IMPLICIT DOUBLE PRECISION (D,X-Z), INTEGER (N-P)
```

would mean that all names starting with the letters D,X,Y or Z would (unless declared otherwise in type statements) have the type double precision. Similarly the letters I through P, instead of just I through N, will imply integer type. The other letters (A–C, E–H, and Q–W) will still imply real type.

IMPLICIT can be used with character type to specify a default length as well, for example:

```
IMPLICIT CHARACTER*100 (C,Z), CHARACTER*4 (S)
```

But this is not usually of much practical value. As with type statements, the default character length is one.

More than one IMPLICIT statement can be used in a program unit but the same letter must not have its implied type specified more than once. The usual Fortran implied-type rules apply to all initial letters not listed in any IMPLICIT statements. The list of letters given after each type must appear in alphabetical order. IMPLICIT statements normally precede all other specification statements in a program. There is one exception to this: PARAMETER statements may precede them provided that the constants named in them are not affected by the IMPLICIT statement. Note that dummy arguments and function names may be affected by a subsequent IMPLICIT statement. IMPLICIT statements have no effect on intrinsic function names.

Guidelines

There are two diametrically opposed schools of thought on type specification. The first holds that *all* names should have their types specified explicitly. This certainly helps programmers to avoid mistakes, because they have to think more carefully about each item. It also helps the compiler to diagnose errors more easily, especially if the it knows that all names are going to be declared in advance. Some Fortran compilers allow a statement of the form 'IMPLICIT NONE' which makes all names typeless by default and so requires every name to be explicitly typed. Others have a compile-time switch with the same effect. If yours does not you may be able to produce a similar effect by using something like:

```
      IMPLICIT CHARACTER*1000000 (A-Z)
```

near the beginning of each program unit which is likely to cause an error for anything not explicitly typed. One disadvantage of the practice of declaring all names in advance is that the program may become so cluttered with specification statements that it may obscure its structure and algorithm.

The alternative way of working is to make maximum use of implicit types to reduce the number of statements. This means, of course, that the first letter of each name has to be chosen to suit the type, leaving no more than five to be chosen freely: this makes it harder than ever to devise meaningful symbolic names. As a result, Fortran programs often include names like RIMAGE or ISIZE or KOUNT. Clearly type statements are still needed for character type because it is usually necessary to use items of a number of different lengths.

Experience suggests that either system can be satisfactory provided it is used consistently. However, the wholesale reassignment of initial letters with IMPLICIT statements usually increases the chance of making a mistake. IMPLICIT, if used at all, should only reassign one or two rarely-used letters to the less common data types, for example:

```
      IMPLICIT DOUBLE PRECISION (Z), LOGICAL (Q),
     $   COMPLEX (X)
```

It is also prudent to use an identical IMPLICIT statement in each program unit, otherwise type mismatches are more likely to be made in procedure calls.

5.4 Named Constants

The PARAMETER statement can be used to give a symbolic name to any constant. This can be useful in several rather different circumstances.

With constants of nature (such as π) and physical conversion factors (like the number of pounds in a kilogram) it can save typing effort and reduce the risk of error if the actual number is only given once in the program and the name used everywhere else:

```
PARAMETER (PI = 3.14159265, TWOPI = 2.0 * PI)
PARAMETER (HALFPI = PI / 2.0, RTOD = 180.0 / PI)
```

The names PI, TWOPI, etc. can then be used in place of the literal constants elsewhere in the program unit. It is much better to use named constants than variables in such cases as they are given better protection against inadvertent corruption: constants are often protected by hardware. The use of symbolic names rather than numbers can also make the program a little more readable: it is probably harder to work out the significance of a number like 1.570796327 than to deduce the meaning of HALFPI.

Another important application of named constants is for items which are not permanent constants but parameters of a program, i.e. items fixed for the present but subject to alteration at some later date. Named constants are often used to specify array bounds, character-string lengths, and so on. For example:

```
      PARAMETER (MAXR = 100, MAXC = 500,
     $   NPTS = MAXR*MAXC)
      REAL MATRIX(MAXR,MAXC), COLUMN(MAXR), ROW(MAXC)
```

The constants such as MAXR and MAXC can also be used in the executable part of the program, for instance to check that the array subscripts are in range:

```
      IF(NCOL .GT. MAXC .OR. NROW .GT. MAXR) THEN
          STOP 'Matrix is too small'
      ELSE
          MATRIX (NROW, NCOL) = ROW (NCOL)
      END IF
```

If, at some point, the matrix turns out to be too small for your needs then you only have to alter this one PARAMETER statement: everything else will change automatically when the program is recompiled.

The rules for character assignment apply to PARAMETER statements: see section 7.4. In addition a special length specification of ★(★) is permitted which means that the length of item is set to that of the literal constant. The type specification must precede the PARAMETER statement.

49

```
      CHARACTER*(*) LETTER, DIGIT, ALPNUM
      PARAMETER (LETTER = 'ABCDEFGHIJKLMNOPQRSTUVWXYZ',
     $   DIGIT = '0123456789', ALPNUM = LETTER // DIGIT)
      CHARACTER WARN*(*)
      PARAMETER (WARN = 'This matrix is nearly singular')
```

The constant ALPNUM will be 36 characters long and contain all the alphanumeric characters (letters and digits).

Named logical constants also exist, but useful applications for them are somewhat harder to find:

```
      PARAMETER (NX=100, NY=200, NZ=300,
     $   NTOT=NX*NY*NZ)
      LOGICAL LARGE
      PARAMETER (LARGE = (NTOT .GT. 1000000) .OR.
     $   (NZ GT. 1000))
```

PARAMETER statement

The general form of the PARAMETER statement is:

PARAMETER (*cname* = *cexp*, *cname* = *cexp*, ...)

where each *cname* is a symbolic name which becomes the name of a constant, and each *cexp* is a *constant expression* of a suitable data type.

The terms in a *constant expression* can only be literal constants or named constants defined earlier in the same program unit. Variables, array elements and function references are not permitted at all. Otherwise the usual rules for expressions apply: parentheses can be used around sub-expressions, and the arithmetic types can be intermixed. There is one restriction on exponentiation: it can only be used to raise a number to an integer power. The normal rules for assignment statements apply: for arithmetic types suitable conversions will be applied if necessary; character strings will be truncated or padded to the required length. Note that substring references are not permitted in character constant expressions.

PARAMETER statements are specification statements and may precede or follow type statements. But any type (or IMPLICIT) statement which affects the data type or length of a named constant must precede it. Subject to these rules, PARAMETER statements are permitted to precede IMPLICIT statements. This makes it possible for a named constant to set the default length for the character type for certain ranges of initial letters. For example:

```
      PROGRAM CLEVER
      PARAMETER (LENCD = 40, LENE = 2 * LENCD)
      IMPLICIT CHARACTER*(LENCD)(C-D),
     $   CHARACTER*(LENE)(E)
      PARAMETER (DEMO = 'This is exactly 40 chars
     $   long')
```

Once defined, a named constant can be used in any expression, including a dimension-bound expression, or in a DATA statement. A named constant cannot be used just as part of another constant (for example one component of a complex constant) and named constants are not permitted at all within format specifications.

Guidelines

One of the limitations of Standard Fortran at present is that there is no way of allocating memory dynamically. One of the best ways around this is to use named constants to specify array bounds; this makes it much easier to alter programs to suit new requirements.

Names should also be given to all mathematical and physical constants that your programs require. If the same constants are needed in several program units then it may be sensible to compose a suitable set of PARAMETER statements for all of them and bring them in wherever necessary using INCLUDE statements.

If you define double precision constants in a PARAMETER statement do not forget that each literal constant value must include an exponent using the letter D.

There are no constant arrays in Fortran: the only way to overcome this limitation is to declare an ordinary array in a type statement and initialise its elements with a DATA statement (described in Chapter 11).

5.5 Variables

A variable is simply a named memory location with a fixed data type. As explained earlier, variables do not have to be declared in advance if the data type implied by the first letter of the name is appropriate. Otherwise a type statement is required.

At the start of execution the value of each variable is undefined unless a suitable DATA statement appears in the program unit (see Chapter 11). Undefined values must not be used in expressions. Local variables in procedures do not necessarily retain their values from one invocation of the procedure to another unless a suitable SAVE statement is provided (section 9.11).

5.6 Arrays

An *array* is a group of memory locations given a single name. The *elements* of the array all have the same data type.

In mathematics the elements of an array *a* would be denoted by a_1, a_2, a_3, and so on. In Fortran a particular array element is identified by providing a *subscript expression* in parentheses after the array name: A(1), A(2), A(3), etc. Subscripts must have integer type but they may be specified by expressions of arbitrary complexity, including function calls.

An array element can be used in the same way as a variable in almost all executable statements. Array elements are most often used within loops: typically an integer loop counter selects each element of the array in turn.

```
*Add   array OLD to array NEW making array TOTAL
       PARAMETER (NDATA = 1024)
       REAL OLD(NDATA), NEW(NDATA), TOTAL(NDATA)
*......
       DO 100, I = 1,NDATA
          TOTAL(I) = OLD(I) + NEW(I)
100    CONTINUE
```

Declaring arrays

Arrays can have up to seven dimensions; the lower bound of each dimension is one unless declared otherwise. There is no limit on the upper bound provided it is not less than the lower bound. Arrays which are dummy arguments of a procedure may have their dimension bounds specified by integer variables which are arguments of the procedure; in all other cases each dimension bound must be an integer constant expression. This fixes the size of the array at compile-time.

Type, DIMENSION and COMMON statements may all be used to declare arrays, but COMMON statements have a specialised use (described in Chapter 12). The DIMENSION statement has a similar form to a *type* statement but only declares the bounds of an array without determining its data type. It is usually simpler and neater to use a *type* statement which specifies both at once:

```
       CHARACTER COLUMN(5)*25, TITLE*80
```

Note that when declaring character arrays the string length follows the list of array bounds. The character array COLUMN has 5 elements each of which is 25 characters long; TITLE is, of course, just a variable 80 characters long. Although a default string length can be set for an entire type statement, it is not possible to set a default array size in a similar way.

It is generally good practice to use named constants to specify array bounds as this facilitates later modifications:

```
PARAMETER (MAXIM = 15)
INTEGER POINTS(MAXIM)
COMPLEX SERIES(2**MAXIM)
```

These arrays all have a lower bound of one. A different lower bound can be specified for any dimension as shown below. The lower and upper bounds are separated by a colon:

```
REAL TAX(1985:1990), PAY(12,1985:1990)
LOGICAL TRIPLE(-1:1, -1:1, -1:1, -1:1)
```

TAX has 6 elements from TAX(1985) to TAX(1990).
PAY has 72 elements from PAY(1,1985) to PAY(12,1990).
TRIPLE has 81 elements from BIN(-1,-1,-1,-1) to BIN(1,1,1,1).

Although Fortran itself sets no limits to the sizes of arrays that can be defined, the finite capacity of the hardware is likely to do so. In *virtual memory* operating systems it is possible to use arrays larger than physical memory: those parts of the array not in active use are held on backing store such as a disk file.

Using arrays

An array element reference must always use the same number of subscripts as the number of dimensions declared for the array. Each subscript can be an integer expression of any complexity, but there are restrictions on using functions with side effects (see section 9.3).

An array element reference is only valid if all of the subscript expressions are defined and if each one is in the range declared for it. An array element can only be used in an expression if a value for it has been defined. A DATA statement (Chapter 12) can be used to define an initial value for an entire array or any set of elements.

An array can be used without subscripts:

- in a specification statement such as a type, DIMENSION, or SAVE statement.
- in a function reference or CALL statement: this transfers the whole of the array to the associated dummy argument (which must have a compatible array declaration).

- in the data transfer list of a READ or WRITE statement: this causes the whole array to be input or output. This is not permitted for an *assumed size* dummy argument array.
- as a unit identifier in a READ or WRITE statement: a character array is then an internal file with one record per element.
- as a format identifier in a READ or WRITE statement: the format specification is contained in the character array with its elements taken in sequence.

Storage sequence

Arrays are always stored in a contiguous set of memory locations. In the case of multi-dimensional arrays, the order of the elements is that the first subscript varies most rapidly, then the second subscript, and so on. For example in the following 2-dimensional array (for simplicity one of only six elements):

$$X(2,3) = \begin{vmatrix} x_{1,1} & x_{1,2} & x_{1,3} \\ x_{2,1} & x_{2,2} & x_{2,3} \end{vmatrix}$$

the elements are stored in the following sequence:

X(1,1), X(2,1), X(1,2), X(2,2), X(1,3), X(2,3),

i.e. the sequence moves down each column first, then across to the next row. This column order is different from that used in some other programming languages.

The storage order may be important if you use large multi-dimensional arrays and wish to carry out some operation on all the elements of the array. It is then likely to be faster to access the array in storage order, i.e. by columns rather than rows. This means arranging loop indices with the last subscript indexed by the outer loop, and so on inwards. For example:

```
        DOUBLE PRECISION ARRAY(100,100), SUM
        SUM = 0.0D0
        DO 250,L = 1,100
            DO 150,K = 1,100
                SUM = SUM + ARRAY(K,L)
150         CONTINUE
250     CONTINUE
```

With the loops arranged this way round the memory locations are accessed in consecutive order, which minimises the processor overhead in subscript calculations.

6 Arithmetic

Fortran has good facilities for processing numbers. Arithmetic expressions and assignment statements can include integer, real, double precision or complex items. Data type conversions are provided automatically when necessary; type conversions can also be performed explicitly using intrinsic functions. Other intrinsic functions are available for trigonometry, logarithms and other useful operations.

For example, the well-known cosine formula for the third side of a triangle, given the other two sides and the angle between them is:

$[b^2 + c^2 - 2bc \cos(A)]^{1/2}$

Translated into a Fortran expression it looks like this:

    SQRT(B**2 + C**2 - 2.0 * B * C * COS(ANGLEA))

which makes use of the intrinsic functions SQRT and COS. Although SQRT(X) produces the same result as X**0.5, the square-root function is simpler, faster, and probably more accurate than raising to the power of one half, which would actually be carried out using both the EXP and LOG functions.

Assignment statements evaluate an expression and assign its value to a variable (or array element). Unlike almost all other Fortran statements, they do not start with a keyword. For example:

    A = SQRT(B**2 + C**2 - 2.0 * B * C * COS(ANGLEA))
    TOTAL(N/2+1) = 0.0
    FLUX = FLUX + 1.0

6.1 Arithmetic Expressions

An expression in its simplest form is just a single *operand*, such as a constant or variable. More complicated expressions combine various operands with *operators*, which specify the computations to be performed. For example:

    RATE * HOURS + BONUS

The rules of Fortran have been designed to resemble those of

55

mathematics as far as possible, especially in determining the order in which the expression is evaluated. In this example the multiplication would always be carried out before the addition, not because it comes first, but because it has a *higher precedence*. When in doubt, or to override the precedence rules, parentheses can be used:

```
(ROOM + DINNER) * 1.15
```

Sub-expressions enclosed in parentheses are always evaluated first; they can be nested to any reasonable depth. If in doubt, there is no harm in adding parentheses to determine the order of evaluation or to make a complicated expression easier to understand.

Arithmetic expressions can contain any of the five arithmetical operators

```
    +    -    *    /    **
```

The double asterisk represents exponentiation, i.e. raising a number to a power. Thus the mathematical expression:

$$(1 + \text{RATE}/100)^{\text{years}}$$

could be represented in Fortran as:

```
(1.0 + RATE/100.0)**YEARS
```

(note the explicit decimal points in the constants to make them real values).

Arithmetic expressions can involve operands of different data types: the data type of the result is determined by some simple rules explained below.

General rules

Arithmetic expressions can contain arithmetic operands, arithmetic operators, and parentheses. There must always be at least one operand. The operands can belong to any of the four arithmetic data types (integer, real, double precision, or complex); the result also has an arithmetic data type. Operands can be any of the following:

- unsigned literal constants
- named constants
- variables
- array elements
- function references
- complete expressions enclosed in parentheses.

The rules for forming more complicated arithmetic expressions are as follows. An *arithmetic expression* can have any of the following forms:

operand
+ *operand*
− *operand*
arithmetic-expression   arith-op   operand

where the *arith-op* can be any of these operators:

+ addition
− subtraction
★ multiplication
/ division
★★ exponentiation

The effect of these rules is that an expression consists of a string of operands separated by operators and, optionally, a plus or minus at the start. A leading plus sign has no effect; a leading minus sign negates the value of the expression.

All literal arithmetical constants used in expressions must be *unsigned*: this is to prevent the use of two consecutive operators which is confusing and possibly ambiguous:

4 / -3.0★★-1 (illegal).

The way around this is to use parentheses, for example:

4 / (-3.0)★★(-1)

which makes the order of evaluation explicit.
The order of evaluation of an expression is:

(1) sub-expressions in parentheses
(2) function references
(3) exponentiation, i.e. raising to a power
(4) multiplication and division
(5) addition, subtraction, or negation.

Within each of these groups evaluation proceeds from left to right, except that exponentiations are evaluated from right to left. Thus:

A / B / C   is equivalent to   (A / B) / C
whereas   X ★★ Y ★★ Z   is equivalent to   X ★★ (Y ★★ Z).

An expression does not have to be evaluated fully if its value can be determined otherwise: for example the result of:

    X ★ FUNC(G)

can be determined without calling the function FUNC if X happens to be zero. This will not cause problems if you only use functions that have no side effects.

Data type conversions

If an operator has two operands of the same data type then the result has the same type. If the operands have different data types then an implicit type conversion is applied to one of them to bring it to the type of the other. These conversions always go in the direction which minimises loss of information:

   integer ⟶ *real* ⟶ *complex* or *double precision*

Since there is no way of converting a complex number to double precision type, or vice versa, without losing significant information, both these conversions are prohibited: an operator cannot have one complex operand and one of double precision type. All other combinations are permitted. These implicit type conversions have the same result as if the appropriate intrinsic function (REAL, DBLE or CMPLX) had been used. These are described in detail below. Note that the data type of any operation just depends on the two operands involved; the rest of the expression has no influence on it whatever.

Exponentiation is an exception to the type conversion rule: when the exponent is an integer it does not have to be converted to the type of the other operand and the result is evaluated as if by repeated multiplication. But if the exponent has any other data type the calculation is performed by implicit use of the LOG and EXP functions, thus:

    2.0★★3   ⟶   2.0 ★ 2.0 ★ 2.0   ⟶   8.0
    2.0★★3.0   ⟶   EXP(3.0 ★ LOG(2.0))   ⟶   8.0

The first result will, of course, be computed more rapidly and accurately than the second. If the exponent has a negative value the result is simply the reciprocal of the corresponding positive power, thus:

    2.0★★(−3)   ⟶   1.0/2.0★★3   ⟶   1.0/8.0   ⟶   0.125

Note that conversion from real to double precision cannot produce any information not present originally. Thus with a real variable R and a double precision variable D:

```
R = 1.0 / 3.0
D = R
```

D may end up with a value such as 0.3333333432674408... which is no closer to the value of one third than R was originally.

Integer division

Integer division always produces a result which is another integer value: any fractional part is truncated, i.e. rounded towards zero. This makes it especially important to provide a decimal point at the end of a real constant even if the fractional part is zero. For example:

8 / 3	$\longrightarrow$	2			
−8 / 3	$\longrightarrow$	−2			
2★★(−3)	$\longrightarrow$	1/(2★★3)	$\longrightarrow$	1/8	$\longrightarrow$ 0

The combination of the two preceding rules may have unexpected effects, for example:

(−2)★★3 $\longrightarrow$ −2 ★ −2 ★ −2 $\longrightarrow$ −8

whereas (−2)★★3.0 is an invalid expression as the computer would try to evaluate the logarithm of -2.0, which does not exist. Similarly, the expression:

3 / 4 ★ 5.0 $\longrightarrow$ REAL(3/4) ★ 5.0 $\longrightarrow$ 0.0

whereas

5.0 ★ 3 / 4 $\longrightarrow$ 15.0 / REAL(4) $\longrightarrow$ 3.75

Restrictions

Certain arithmetical operations are prohibited because their results are not mathematically defined. For example dividing by zero, raising a negative value to a real power, and raising zero to a negative power. The Fortran Standard does not specify exactly what is to happen if one of these errors occurs: most systems issue an error message and abort the program.

Errors can also occur because numbers are stored on a computer with finite range and precision. The results of adding or multiplying two very large numbers may be outside the number range: this is called *overflow*. A similar effect on very large negative integers is called *underflow*. Most systems will issue a warning message for overflow or underflow, and may abort the program, but some processors cannot detect errors of this sort involving integer arithmetic.

Every operand (variable, array element, or function reference) used in an expression must have a defined value at the time the expression is evaluated. Note that variables and arrays are initially undefined unless a suitable DATA statement is used.

Expressions must not include references to any external functions with side effects on other operands of the same expression: see section 9.3 for more details.

Arithmetic constant expressions

Arithmetic constant expressions can be used in PARAMETER statements and to specify implied-DO parameters in DATA statements. All the operands in a constant expression must be literal constants or previously defined named constants. Variables, array elements, and function references are all prohibited. Exponentiation is only allowed if the number is raised to an integer power.

The same rules apply to integer constant expressions but, in addition, the operands must all be integer constants: such expressions can be used to specify array bounds in *type*, COMMON and DIMENSION statements, and to specify string lengths in CHARACTER statements.

Bit-wise logical operations

When Fortran programs communicate directly with digital hardware it may be necessary to carry out bit-wise logical operations on bit-patterns. Standard Fortran does not provide any direct way of doing this, since logical variables essentially store only one bit of information and integer variables can only be used for arithmetic. Many systems provide, as an extension, intrinsic functions to perform bit-wise operations on integers. The function names vary: typically they are IAND, IOR, ISHIFT. A few systems allow the normal logical operators such as .AND. and .OR. to be used with integer arguments: this is a much more radical extension and much less satisfactory, because it not only reduces portability, but also reduces the ability of the compiler to detect errors in normal arithmetic expressions.

Many systems also provide format descriptors to transfer integers using octal and hexadecimal number bases: these are also non-standard.

Guidelines

Expressions with mixed data types should be examined carefully to ensure that the type-conversion rules have the desired effect. It does no harm to use the type conversion functions explicitly and it may make the working clearer.

Particular care is needed with the data types of literal constants. It is bad practice to use an integer constant where you really need a real constant. Although this will work in most *expressions* it is a serious mistake to use the wrong form of constant in the argument list of a procedure.

Long and complicated expressions which spread over several lines can be rather trying to read and offer more scope for programming errors. Sometimes it is better to split the computation into several shorter equations at the expense of one or two temporary variables.

It is often tempting to try to write programs that are as efficient as possible. With modern compilers there is little point in trying to rearrange expressions to optimise speed. One of the few exceptions is that if an intrinsic function is provided it is always best to use it; thus SQRT(X) is likely to be faster and more accurate than X**0.5.

You may find that your system actually sets the whole of memory to zero initially, except for items defined with DATA statements, but it is very bad programming practice to rely on this.

6.2 Arithmetic Intrinsic Functions

Intrinsic functions are supplied automatically by the system and can be used in expressions in any program unit. A description of their special properties appears in section 9.1.

Many of the arithmetic intrinsic functions have *generic* names: that is, they can be used with several different types of arguments. The SQRT function, for example, can be used with a real, double precision or complex argument. The Fortran system automatically selects the correct specific function for the job: SQRT, DSQRT or CSQRT. These *specific* names can be ignored in almost all circumstances, and are listed only in Appendix C. In most cases the data type of the function is the same as that of its argument but there are a few obvious exceptions, such as the type conversion functions.

In the descriptions below, the number and data type of the arguments of each intrinsic function are indicated by a letter:

| I = | integer | R = real, |
| D = | double precision | Cx = complex |

An asterisk on the left indicates that the result has the same data type as the arguments. Note that if multiple arguments are permitted they must all have the same data type. Thus I = NINT(RD) indicates that the NINT function can take a single real or double precision argument but its result is always integer, whereas ★ = ANINT(RD) indicates that the result has the same type (real or double precision) as the argument.

Trigonometric functions

The functions in this group can all be used on real or double precision arguments, SIN and COS can also be used on complex numbers. In every case the result has the same data type as the argument.

★ = SIN(RDCx)	Sine of the angle in radians.
★ = COS(RDCx)	Cosine of the angle in radians.
★ = TAN(RD)	Tangent of the angle in radians.
★ = ASIN(RD)	Arc-sine; the result is in the range $-\pi/2$ to $+\pi/2$.
★ = ACOS(RD)	Arc-cosine; the result is in the range 0 to $+\pi$.
★ = ATAN(RD)	Arc-tangent; the result is in the range $-\pi/2$ to $+\pi/2$.
★ = ATAN2(RD,RD)	Arc-tangent of A_1/A_2; the result is in the range $-\pi$ to $+\pi$. Both arguments must not be zero.
★ = SINH(RD)	Hyperbolic sine.
★ = COSH(RD)	Hyperbolic cosine.
★ = TANH(RD)	Hyperbolic tangent.

Note that the arguments of SIN, COS and TAN must be angles measured in radians (not degrees). They can be used on angles of any size, positive or negative, but if the magnitude is very large the accuracy of the result will be reduced. Similarly, all the inverse trigonometric functions deliver a result in radians; the argument of ASIN and ACOS must be in the range −1 to +1.

The ATAN2 function can be useful in resolving a result into the correct quadrant of the circle, thus:

ATAN(0.5) = 0.4636476
ATAN2(2.0,4.0) = 0.4636476
ATAN2(−2.0,−4.0) = −2.677945 (= 0.4636476 − π).

Other transcendental functions

★ = SQRT(RDCx)   Square root.
★ = LOG(RDCx)   Natural logarithm, i.e. log to base e (where e = 2.718281828...).
★ = EXP(RDCx)   Returns the exponential, i.e. e to the power of the argument. This is the inverse of the natural logarithm.
★ = LOG10(RD)   Logarithm to base 10.

Note that LOG10, which may be useful to compute decibel ratios etc., is the only one of this group which cannot be used on a complex argument.

Type conversion functions

These functions can be used to convert from any of the four arithmetic data types to any of the others. They are used automatically whenever mixed data types are encountered in arithmetic expressions and assignments.

I − INT(IRDCx)   Converts to integer by truncation.
R = REAL(IRDCx)   Converts to real.
D = DBLE(IRDCx)   Converts to double precision.
Cx = CMPLX(IRD)   Converts to complex.
Cx = CMPLX(IRD,IRD)   Converts to complex.

The integer conversion of INT rounds towards zero; if you need to round to the nearest integer use the NINT function (described below). The CMPLX function produces a value with a zero imaginary component unless it is used with two arguments (or one which is already complex). It is important to realise that many conversions lose information: in particular a double precision value is likely to lose significant digits if converted to any other data type.

Minimum and maximum

The MIN and MAX functions are unique in being able to take any number of arguments from two upwards; the result has the same data type as the arguments.

★ = MIN(IRD,IRD,...)   Returns the smallest of its arguments.
★ = MAX(IRD,IRD,...)   Returns the largest of its arguments.

These two functions can, of course, be combined to limit a value to a certain range. For example, to limit a value TEMPER to the range 32 to 212 you can use an expression such as:

```
MAX(32.0, MIN(TEMPER, 212.0))
```

Note that the minimum of the range is an argument of the MAX function and vice versa.

To find the largest (or smallest) element of a large array it is necessary use a loop.

```
*Find largest value in array T of N elements:
     TOP = T(1)
     DO 25,I = 2,N
        TOP = MAX(T(I),TOP)
25   CONTINUE
*TOP now contains the largest element of T.
```

Other functions

★ =	AINT(RD)	Truncates the fractional part (i.e. as INT) but preserves the data type.
★ =	ANINT(RD)	Rounds to the nearest whole number.
I =	NINT(RD)	Converts to integer by rounding to the nearest whole number.
★ =	ABS(IRD)	Returns the absolute value of a number (i.e. it changes the sign if negative).
R =	ABS(Cx)	Computes the modulus of a complex number (i.e. the square-root of the sum of the squares of the two components).
★ =	MOD(IRD,IRD)	Returns A_1 modulo A_2, i.e. the remainder after dividing A_1 by A_2.
★ =	SIGN(IRD,IRD)	Performs sign transfer: if A_2 is negative the result is $-A_1$, if A_2 is zero or positive the result is A_1.
★ =	DIM(IRD,IRD)	Returns the positive difference of A_1 and A_2, i.e. if $A_1 > A_2$ it returns (A_1-A_2), otherwise zero.

D = DPROD(R,R)   Computes the double precision product of two real values.
R = AIMAG(Cx)   Extracts the imaginary component of a complex number. Note that the real component can be obtained by using the REAL function.
Cx = CONJG(Cx)   Computes the complex conjugate of a complex number.

The NINT and ANINT functions round upwards if the fractional part of the argument is 0.5 or more, whereas INT and AINT always round towards zero. Thus:

INT(+3.5) = 3   NINT(+3.5) = 4
INT(−3.5) = −3   NINT(−3.5) = −4

The fractional part of a floating point number, X, can easily be found either by:

    X - AINT(X)

or

    MOD(X, 1.0)

In either case, if X is negative the result will also be negative. The ABS function can always be used to alter the sign if required.

The MOD function has other uses. For example, it can find the day of the week from an absolute day count such as Modified Julian Date (MJD):

    MOD(MJD,7)

has a value between 0 and 6 for days from Wednesday to Tuesday. Similarly if you use the ATAN2 function but want the result to lie in the range 0 to 2π (rather than $-\pi$ to $+\pi$) then, assuming the value of TWOPI is suitably defined, the required expression is:

    MOD(ATAN2(X,Y) + TWOPI, TWOPI)

6.3 Arithmetic Assignment Statements

An arithmetic assignment statement has the form:

    arithmetic-var = *arithmetic-expression*

where *arithmetic-var* can be an arithmetic variable or array element.

For example, the following assignment statement is valid provided that N, K and ANGLE are all defined values:

```
IMAGE (N/2+1, 3*K-1) = SIN (ANGLE)**2 + 1.0
```

If the object on the left has a different data type from that of the expression on the right then a data type conversion is applied automatically. The type conversion function (INT, REAL, DBLE or CMPLX) is selected to match the object on the left. Note that many type conversions lose information. If the object on the left is an array element, its subscripts can be arbitrary integer expressions, but all the operands in these expressions must be defined before the statement is executed and each must be in the range declared for the corresponding subscript of the array.

Remember: with an integer item on the left and an expression of one of the floating-point types, the INT function is invoked; if the NINT function is actually needed then it must be used explicitly.

7 Character Handling and Logic

This chapter describes the facilities for handling non-numerical data in Fortran. Character data are actually present in almost all programs, if only in the form of file names and error messages, but the facilities for character manipulation are now quite powerful. The logical data type is also indispensible since a logical expression is used in every IF statement.

7.1 Character Facilities

The character data type differs from all the others in one important respect: every character item has a fixed length. This specifies the number of characters it holds.

The length of a literal character constant is just the number of characters between the enclosing apostrophes (except that two consecutive apostrophe within the string count as one). Thus:

    'it''s'

is a character constant of length four. Because the length of every character variable, array and function has to be specified in advance it is nearly always necessary to use CHARACTER statements to declare them, for example:

    CHARACTER NAME*20, ADDRSS(3)*40, ZIP*7

The same applies to named character constants but for these a special notation sets the length to that of the attached constant, which saves the trouble of counting characters:

    CHARACTER TITLE*(*)
    PARAMETER (TITLE = 'Latest mailing list')

The fixed length of character objects makes it easy to output data in a fixed format as when printing a table with neatly aligned columns, but sometimes it would be more convenient to have a variable length string type as some other languages do. The rules for character assignment go some way towards this: if an expression is too short then blanks are appended to it; if it is too long then characters are removed from the right-hand end. For many purposes, therefore, it is only necessary to ensure that character variables are at least as long as the longest string you need to store in them.

When transferring character information to procedures the length of the dummy argument can be set automatically to that of the corresponding actual argument. With this *passed length* notation it is easy to write general-purpose character handling procedures. This is described further in section 9.5.

The most common operations carried out on character strings are splitting them up and joining them together. Any section of a character variable or array element can be extracted by using the *substring* notation. Strings (and substrings) can be joined end to end by using the concatenation operator in a character expression. These are described in the next two sections.

Another fairly common requirement is to search for a particular sequence of characters within a longer string: this can be done with the intrinsic function INDEX.

Other intrinsic functions, ICHAR and CHAR, are provided to convert a single character to an integer or vice versa according to its position within the native character set. More complicated conversions from a numerical data type to character form and vice versa are best carried out using the *internal file* READ and WRITE statements which allow the power of the *format specification* to be applied to the task. This mechanism is described in section 10.3.

Character strings can be compared to each other using relational operators or intrinsic functions. The latter use the ASCII collating sequence irrespective of the native character code. Further details are given in section 7.6.

7.2 Character Substrings

The substring notation can be used to select any contiguous section of any character variable or array element. The characters in any string are numbered starting from one on the left: the lower bound cannot be altered as it can in arrays. A substring is selected simply by giving the first and last character positions of the extract. For example, with:

```
CHARACTER METAL*10
METAL = 'CADMIUM'
```

then

METAL(1:3)   has the value 'CAD'
METAL(8:8)   has the value '   ' because the value is padded out with blanks to its declared length.

Substrings must be at least one character long. They can be used in general in the same ways as character variables. Continuing with the last example, the assignment statement:

METAL(3:4) = 'ES'

will change the value of METAL to 'CAESIUM   ' (with three blanks at the end, since the total length stays at 10).

Substring rules

The parentheses denoting a substring must contain a colon: there may be an integer expression on either side of the colon. The first expression denotes the initial character position, the second one the last character position. Both values must be within the range 1 to LEN, where LEN is the length of the parent string, and the length of the resulting substring must not be less than one.

Although the colon must always be present, the two integer expressions are optional. The default value for the first one is one, the default for the second is the position of the last character of the parent string. Thus, staying with the last example:

METAL(:2)   has the value 'CA'
METAL(7:)   has the value ' M   '   with three blanks.

With array elements the substring expression follows the sub-script expression, for example:

CHARACTER PLAY(30)*80
PLAY(10) = 'AS YOU LIKE IT'

Then the substring

PLAY(10) (4:11)   has the value 'YOU LIKE'.

Substrings can be used in expressions anywhere except in the definition of a statement function; they can also be used on the left-hand side of an assignment statement and can also be defined by input/output statements.

7.3 Character Expressions

The character operator // is used to concatenate, or join, two character strings. It is, in fact, the only character operator that Fortran provides. Thus:

'CUP' // 'BOARD' $\longrightarrow$ 'CUPBOARD'

The length of the result is just the sum of the lengths of the operands. Parentheses may be used in character expressions but make no difference to the result. Note that any embedded or trailing blanks (spaces) will be reproduced exactly in the resulting string.

The general form of a *character-expression* is thus:

character-operand

or

character-expression // character-operand

where *character-operand* can be any of the following:

- character constant (literal or named).
- character variable,
- character array element,
- character substring,
- character function reference.

There is one special restriction on character concatenation in procedures: a passed-length dummy argument can only be an operand of the concatenation operator in an assignment statement. This seemingly arbitrary rule allows the compiler to determine how much workspace is required.

7.4 Character Assignment Statements

The character assignment statement has the general form:

char-var = character-expression

where *char-var* can be a character variable, array element or substring.

There is one important restriction on character assignment statements: none of the characters being referenced in the expression on the right may be defined in *char-var* on the left, that is to say there can be no overlap. Thus the assignment statement:

```
STRING(1:N) = STRING(10:)
```

is valid only as long as N is no higher than 9. It is, of course, easy to get around this restriction by using a temporary character variable with a suitable length.

Note that when a value is assigned to a substring (as in the last example) the other characters in the parent string are not affected at all. If the string was previously undefined then the other character positions will still be undefined; otherwise they will retain their previous contents.

The expression and the character object to which its value is assigned may have different lengths: if the expression is longer, then the excess characters on the right are lost; if it is shorter, then blanks are appended. Care is needed to declare adequate lengths or else the results can be unexpected:

```
CHARACTER AUTHOR*30, SHORT*5, EXPAND*10
AUTHOR = 'SHAKESPEARE, WILLIAM'
SHORT = AUTHOR
EXPAND = SHORT
```

The resulting value of EXPAND will be 'SHAKE △△△△△' where the last five characters are blanks.

7.5 Character Intrinsic Functions

The four main character intrinsic functions are described in this section. There are another four functions provided to compare character strings with each other using the ASCII collating sequence: these are described in section 7.6.

CHAR and ICHAR

These two functions perform integer to character conversion and vice versa using the internal code of the machine. Although most computers now use the ASCII character code, it is by no means universal, so these functions can only be used in a very limited way in portable software.

CHAR(I) returns the character at position I in the code table. For example, on a machine using ASCII code, CHAR(74) = 'J', since 'J' is the character number 74 in the ASCII code table.

ICHAR(STRING) returns the integer position in the code table of the first character of the argument STRING. For example, on a machine using ASCII code,

ICHAR('JOHN') ⟶ 74
ICHAR('john') ⟶ 106

INDEX

INDEX is a search function; it takes two character arguments and returns an integer result. INDEX(S_1, S_2) searches for the character-string S_2 in another string S_1, which is usually longer. If S_2 is present in S_1 the function returns the character position at which it starts. If there is no match (or S_1 is shorter than S_2) then it returns the value zero. For example:

```
CHARACTER*20 SPELL
SPELL    = 'ABRACADABRA'
K        = INDEX(SPELL, 'RA')
```

Here K will be set to 3 because this is the position of the first occurrence of the string 'RA'. To find the second occurrence it is necessary to restart the search at the next character in the main string, for example:

```
L = INDEX(SPELL(K+1:), 'RA')
```

This will return the value 7 because the first occurrence of 'RA' in the substring 'ACADABRA' is at position 7. To find its position in the parent string the offset, K, must be added, making 10.

The INDEX function is often useful when manipulating character information. Suppose, for example, we have a string NAME containing a person's surname and initials, e.g.

   Mozart,W.A.

The name can be reformatted to put the initials before the surname and omit the comma like this:

```
      CHARACTER NAME*25, PERSON*25
*...
      KCOMMA = INDEX(NAME, ',')
      KSPACE = INDEX(NAME, ' ')
      PERSON = NAME(KCOMMA+1:KSPACE-1) //
     $         NAME(1:KCOMMA-1)
```

Then PERSON will contain the string 'W.A.Mozart' (with blanks appended to the length of 25). Note that a separate variable, PERSON, was necessary because of the rule about overlapping strings in assignments.

LEN

The LEN function takes a character argument and returns its length as an integer. The argument may be a local character variable or array element but this will just return a constant. LEN is more useful in procedures where character dummy arguments (and character function names) may have their length passed over from the calling unit, so that the length may be different on each procedure call. The length returned by LEN is that declared for the item. Sometimes it is more useful to find the length excluding trailing blanks. The next function does just that, using LEN in the process.

```
      INTEGER FUNCTION LENGTH(STRING)
*Returns length of string ignoring trailing blanks
      CHARACTER*(*) STRING
      DO 15, I = LEN(STRING), 1, -1
         IF(STRING(I:I) .NE. ' ') GO TO 20
15    CONTINUE
20    LENGTH = I
      END
```

7.6 Relational Expressions

A relational expression compares the values of two arithmetic expressions or two character expressions: the result is a logical value, either true or false. Relational expressions are commonly used in IF statements, as in this example:

```
      IF(SENSOR .GT. UPPER) THEN
         CALL COOL
      ELSE IF(SENSOR .LT. LOWER) THEN
         CALL HEAT
      END IF
```

The relational operators have forms such as .GT. and .LT. because the Fortran character set does not include the usual characters > and <. Relational expressions are most commonly used in IF statements, but any logical variable or array element may be used to store a logical value for use later on.

```
      CHARACTER*10 OPTION
      LOGICAL EXIT
      EXIT = OPTION .EQ. 'FINISH'
*...
      IF(EXIT) STOP 'Finish requested'
```

Logical expressions are covered in more detail in the next section.

General forms of relational expression

>   *arithmetic-exprn   rel-op   arithmetic-exprn*

or

>   *character-exprn   rel-op   character-exprn*

In either case the resulting expression has the *logical* type. The relational operator *rel-op* can be any of the following:

- .EQ.   equal to
- .GE.   greater than or equal to
- .GT.   greater than
- .LE.   less than or equal to
- .LT.   less than
- .NE.   not equal to

Note that these operators need a decimal point at either end to distinguish them from symbolic names.

Arithmetic comparisons

When the two arithmetic values of differing data type are compared, a conversion is automatically applied to one of them (as in arithmetic expressions) to bring it to the type of the other. The direction of conversion is always:

>   integer $\longrightarrow$ real $\longrightarrow$ complex or double precision.

When comparing integer expressions, there is a considerable difference between the .LE. and .LT. operators, and similarly between .GE. and .GT., so that you should consider carefully what action is required in the limiting case before selecting the appropriate operator.

In comparisons involving the other arithmetic types you should remember that the value of a number may not be stored exactly. This means that it is unwise to rely on tests involving the .EQ. and .NE. operators except in special cases; for example, if one of the values has previously been set to zero or some other small integer.

There are two restrictions on complex values: firstly they cannot be compared at all to values of double precision type; secondly they cannot use relational operators other than .EQ. and .NE. because there is no simple linear ordering of complex numbers.

Character comparisons

A character value can only be compared to another character value; if they do not have the same length then the shorter one is padded out with blanks to the length of the other before the comparison takes place. Tests for equality (or inequality) do not depend on the character code; the two strings are just compared character by character until a difference is found. Comparisons using the other operators (.GE., .GT., .LE. and .LT.) do, however, depend on the local character code. The two expressions are compared one character position at a time until a difference is found: the result then depends on the relative positions of the two characters in the local collating sequence, i.e. the order in which the characters appear in the character code table.

The Fortran Standard specifies that the collating sequence used by all systems must have the following basic properties:

- All the upper-case letters are in order, A < B < C etc.
- All digits are in order, 0 < 1 < 2 etc.
- All digits precede all letters or vice versa.
- The blank (space) character precedes letters and digits.

It does not, however, specify whether letters precede digits or follow them. As a result, if strings of mixed text are sorted using relational operators the results may be machine dependent. For example, the expression

    'APPLE' .LT. 'APRICOT'

is always *true* because the two strings first differ at the third character position, and the letter 'P' precedes 'R' in all Fortran collating sequences. However:

    'A1' .GT. 'AONE'

will have a value *true* if your system uses EBCDIC but *false* if it uses ASCII, because the digits follow letters in the former and precede them in the latter.

In order to allow character comparisons to be made in a truly portable way, Fortran has provided four additional intrinsic functions. These perform character comparisons using the ASCII collating sequence no matter what the native character code of the machine. These functions are:

    LGE(S1, S2)   greater than or equal to
    LGT(S1, S2)   greater than
    LLE(S1, S2)   less than or equal to

LLT(S1, S2)   less than.

They take two character arguments (of any length) and return a logical value. Thus the expression:

    LGT('A1', 'AONE')

will always have the value *false*.

Character comparisons are case-sensitive on machines which have lower-case letters in their character set. It is advisable to convert both arguments to the same case beforehand.

Guidelines

Systems which support both upper and lower-case characters are usually case-sensitive: before testing for the presence of particular keywords or commands it is usually best to convert the input string to a standard case, usually upper-case. Unfortunately there are no standard intrinsic functions to do this, though many systems provide them as an extension.

In character sorting operations where the strings contain mixtures of letters, digits or other symbols, you should use the intrinsic functions to make the program portable. In other character comparisons, however, the relational operator notation is probably preferable because it has a more familiar form and may be slightly more efficient.

7.7 Logical Expressions

Logical expressions can be used in logical assignment statements, but are most commonly encountered in IF statements where there is a compound condition, for example:

        IF (AGE .GE. 60 .OR. (STATUS .EQ. 'WIDOW' .AND
    $ NCHILD .GT. 0) THEN

This combines the values of three relational expressions, two of them comparing arithmetic values, the other character values. The logical operators such as .AND. and .OR. also need decimal points at either end to distinguish them from symbolic names. The .OR. operator performs an inclusive *or*, the *exclusive or* operator is called .NEQV..

Rules

A *logical expression* can have any of the following forms:

logical-term
.NOT. *logical-term*
logical-expression   logical-operator   logical-term

Where: *logical term* can be any of the following:

- Logical constant (literal or named).
- Logical variable.
- Logical array element.
- Logical function reference.
- Logical expression enclosed in parentheses.
- Relational expression.

and the *logical operator* can be any of the following:

.AND.	logical and
.OR.	logical inclusive or
.EQV.	logical equivalence
.NEQV.	logical non-equivalence (i.e. exclusive or).

Note that the rules of logical expressions only allow two successive operators to occur if the second of them is the unary operator .NOT. which negates the value of its operand. The effects of the four binary logical operators are shown in Table 7.1 below for the four possible combinations of operands, x and y.

Table 7.1   Logical operators

x	y	x.AND.y	x.OR.y	x.EQV.y	x.NEQV.Y
false	false	false	false	true	false
true	false	false	true	false	true
false	true	false	true	false	true
true	true	true	true	true	false

Note that a logical expression can have operands which are complete relational expressions, and these can in turn contain arithmetic expressions. The complete order of precedence of the operators in a general expression is as follows:

(1) arithmetical operators (in the order defined in section 6.1 above)
(2) relational operators
(3) .NOT.
(4) .AND.
(5) .OR.
(6) .EQV. and .NEQV.

If the operators .EQV. and .NEQV. are used at the same level in an expression they are evaluated from left to right.

These rules reduce the need for parentheses in logical expressions, thus:

```
(X .GT. A) .OR. (Y .GT. B)
```

would have exactly the same meaning if all the parentheses were omitted.

A Fortran system is not required to evaluate every term in a logical expression if its value can be determined more simply. In the above example, if X had been greater than A then it would not be necessary to compare Y and B for the expression would have been *true* in either case. This improves efficiency but means that functions with side-effects should not be used.

Guidelines

Complicated logical and relational expressions can be hard to read especially if they extend through several successive lines. It helps to line up similar conditions on successive lines and to use parentheses.

7.8 Logical Assignment Statements

A logical assignment statement has the form:

logical-var = *logical-expression*

Where the *logical-var* can be a logical variable or array element. Logical variables and array elements are mainly used to store the values of relational expressions until some later point where they are used in IF statements.

8 Control Statements

Executable statements are normally executed in sequence except as specified by control statements. The END= and ERR= keywords of input/output statements can also affect the execution sequence.

8.1 Control Structures

Branches

The best way to select alternative paths through a program is to use the *block-IF* structure: this may comprise a single block to be executed when a specified condition is true or several blocks to cover several eventualities. Where the IF-block would only contain one statement it is possible to use an abbreviated form called (for historical reasons) the *logical-IF* statement.

There is also a *computed* GO TO statement which can produce a multi-way branch similar to the 'case' statements of other languages.

Loops

Another fundamental requirement is that of repetition. If the number of cycles is known in advance then the DO statement should be used. This also controls a block of statements known as the DO-loop. A CONTINUE statement usually marks the end of a DO-loop.

Fortran has no direct equivalent of the 'do while' and 'repeat until' forms available in some program languages for loops of an indefinite number of iterations, but they can be constructed using simple GO TO and IF statements.

Other control statements

The STOP statement can be used to terminate execution. Other statements which affect execution sequence are described in other chapters: the END statement was covered in section 4.7; procedure calls including the CALL and RETURN statements are described in Chapter 9.

8.2 IF-Blocks

The simplest form of IF-block looks like this:

```
IF(N .NE. 0) THEN
    AVERAG = SUM / N
    AVGSQ = SUMSQ / N
END IF
```

The statements in the block are only executed if the condition is true. In this example the statements in the block are not executed if N is zero in order to avoid division by zero.

The IF-block can also contain an ELSE statement to handle the alternative:

```
IF(B**2 .GE. 4.0 * A * C) THEN
    WRITE(UNIT=*,FMT=*)'Real roots'
ELSE
    WRITE(UNIT=*,FMT=*)'No real roots'
END IF
```

Since the IF statement contains a *logical expression* its value can only be *true* or *false*, thus one or other of these blocks will always be executed.

If there are several alternative conditions to be tested, they can be specified with ELSE IF statements:

```
IF(OPTION .EQ. 'PRINT') THEN
    CALL OUTPUT(ARRAY)
ELSE IF(OPTION .EQ. 'READ') THEN
    CALL INPUT(ARRAY)
ELSE IF(OPTION .EQ. 'QUIT') THEN
    CLOSE(UNIT=OUT)
    STOP 'end of program'
ELSE
    WRITE(UNIT=*,FMT=*)' Error try again...'
END IF
```

There can be any number of ELSE IF blocks but in each case one, and only one, will be executed each time. Without an ELSE block on the end nothing would have happened when an invalid option was selected.

Block-IF general rules

The general form of the block-IF structure is as follows:

```
IF ( logical-expression ) THEN
    a block of
    statements
ELSE IF ( logical-expression ) THEN
    another block of
    statements
ELSE
    a final block of
    statements
END IF
```

The IF THEN, ELSE IF and ELSE statements each govern one block of statements. There can be any number of ELSE IF statements. The ELSE statement (together with its block) is also optional, and there can be at most one of these.

The first block of statements is executed only if the first expression is true. Each block after an ELSE IF is executed only if none of the preceding blocks has been executed and the attached ELSE IF expression is true. If there is an ELSE block it is executed only if none of the preceding blocks has been executed.

After a block has been executed control is transferred to the statement following the END IF statement at the end of the structure (unless the block ends with some statement which transfers control elsewhere).

Any block can contain a complete block-IF structure properly nested within it, or a complete DO-loop, or any other executable statements (except END).

It is illegal to transfer control into any block from outside it, but there is no restriction on transferring control out of a block.

The rules for logical expressions are covered in section 7.7

Guidelines

The indentation scheme shown in the examples above is not mandatory but the practice of indenting each block by a few characters relative to the rest of the program is strongly recommended. It makes the structure of the block immediately apparent and reduces the risk of failing to match each IF with an END IF. An indenting scheme is especially useful when IF-blocks are nested within others. For example:

```
      IF(POWER .GT. LIMIT) THEN
          IF(.NOT. WARNED) THEN
              CALL SET('WARNING')
              WARNED = .TRUE.
          ELSE
              CALL SET('ALARM')
          END IF
      END IF
```

The limited width of the statement field can be a problem when IF-blocks are nested to a very great depth: but this tends to mean that the program unit is getting too complicated and that it will usually be beneficial to divide it into subroutines. If you accidentally omit an END IF statement the compiler will flag the error but will not know where you forgot to put it. In such cases the compiler may get confused and generate a large number of other error messages.

When an IF-block which is executed frequently contains a large number of ELSE IF statements it will be slightly more efficient to put the most-likely conditions near the top of the list as when they occur the tests lower down in the list will not need to be executed.

8.3 DO-Loops

The DO statement controls a block of statements which are executed repeatedly, once for each value of a variable called the loop-control variable. The number of iterations depends on the parameters of the DO statement at the head of the loop. The first item after the keyword 'DO' is the label which is attached to the last statement of the loop. For example:

```
*Sum the squares of the first N elements of the
*array X
      SUM = 0.0
      DO 15, I = 1,N
          SUM = SUM + X(I)**2
15    CONTINUE
```

If we had wanted only to sum alternate elements of the array we could have used a statement like:

```
      DO 15, I = 1,N,2
```

and then the value of I in successive loops would have been 1, 3, 5, etc. The final value would be N if N were odd, or only N-1 if N were even. If the third parameter is omitted the step-size is one; if it is negative then the steps go downwards. For example:

```
        DO 100,I = 5,1,-1
            WRITE(UNIT=*,FMT=*) I**2
100     CONTINUE
```

will produce 5 records containing the values 25, 16, 9, 4 and 1 respectively.

Loops can be nested to any reasonable depth. Thus the following statements will set the two dimensional array FIELD to zero.

```
        REAL FIELD(NX, NY)
        DO 50, IY = 1,NY
            DO 40, IX = 1,NX
                FIELD(IX,IY) = 0.0
40          CONTINUE
50      CONTINUE
```

General form of DO statement

The DO statement has two forms:

        DO *label, variable* = *start, limit, step*

or

        DO *label, variable* = *start, limit*

In the second form the step size is implicitly one.

The *label* marks the final statement of the loop. It must be attached to an executable statement further on in the program unit. The rules permit this statement to be any executable statement except another control statement, but it is strongly recommended that you use the CONTINUE statement here. CONTINUE has no other function except to act as a dummy place-marker.

The comma after the label is optional but, as noted in section 1.4, is a useful precaution.

The variable which follows is known as the *loop control variable* or loop index; it must be a variable (not an array element) but may have integer, real or double precision type.

The *start*, *limit* and *step* values may be expressions of any form of integer, real or double precision type. If the step value is present it must not be zero, if omitted it is taken as one. The number of iterations is computed before the start of the first one, using the formula:

    iterations = MAX(INT(0, (limit − start + step) / step))

Note that if the limit value is less than start, the iteration count is zero unless step is negative. A zero iteration count is permitted but means that the contents of the loop will not be executed at all and control is transferred to the first statement after the end of the loop. The loop control variable does not necessarily reach the limiting value, especially if the step-size is larger than one.

Statements within the loop are permitted to alter the value of the expressions used for start, limit, or step but this has no effect on the iteration count which is fixed before the first iteration starts.

The loop control variable may be used in expressions but a new value must not be assigned to it within the loop.

DO-loops may contain other DO-loops completely nested within them provided that a different loop control variable is used in each one. Although it is permissible for two different loops to terminate on the same statement, this can be very confusing. It is much better to use a separate CONTINUE statement at the end of each loop. Similarly complete IF-blocks may be nested within DO-loops, and vice versa.

Other control statements may be used to transfer control out of the range of a DO-loop but it is illegal to try to jump into a loop from outside it. If you exit from a loop prematurely in this way the loop control variable keeps its current value and may be used outside to determine how many loops were actually executed.

After the normal termination of a DO-loop the loop control variable has the value it had on the last iteration plus one extra increment of the step value. Thus with:

```
        DO 1000, NUMBER = 0,100,3
1000    CONTINUE
```

On the last iteration NUMBER would be 99, and on exit from the loop NUMBER would be 102. This provision can be useful in the event of exit from a loop because of some error:

```
        PARAMETER (MAXVAL = 100)
        REAL X(MAXVAL)
        DO 15, I = 1,MAXVAL
            READ(UNIT=*, FMT=*, END=90) X(I)
15      CONTINUE
90      NVALS = I - 1
```

The action of the statement labelled 90 is to set NVALS to the number of values actually read from the file whether there was a premature exit because the end-of-file was detected or it reached the end of the array space at MAXVAL.

Guidelines

If you use a loop-control variable of any type other than integer there is a risk that rounding errors will accumulate as it is incremented repeatedly. In addition, if the expressions for the start, limit and step values are not of integer type, the number of iterations may not be what you expect because the formula uses the INT function (not NINT). None of these problems can occur if integer quantities are used throughout the DO statement.

8.4 Logical-IF Statement

The logical-IF statement is best regarded as a special case of the IF-block when it only contains one statement. Thus:

```
IF (E .NE. 0.0) THEN
    RECIPE = 1.0 / E
END IF
```

can be replaced by a single logical-IF statement:

```
IF (E .NE. 0.0) RECIPE = 1.0 / E
```

The general form of the logical-IF statement is:

```
IF ( logical-expression ) statement
```

The *statement* is executed only if the logical expression has a true value. Any executable statement is permitted here except DO, IF, ELSE IF, ELSE, END IF, or END.

8.5 Unconditional GO TO Statement

The unconditional GO TO statement simply produces a transfer of control to a labelled executable statement elsewhere in the program unit. Its general form is:

```
GO TO label
```

Note that control must not be transferred into an IF-block or a DO-loop from outside it.

Guidelines

The unconditional GO TO statement makes it possible to construct programs with a very undisciplined structure; such programs are usually hard to understand and to maintain. Good programmers use GO TO statements and labels very sparingly. Unfortunately it is not always possible to avoid them entirely in Fortran because of a lack of alternative control structures.

The next example finds the highest common factor of two integers M and N using a Euclid's algorithm. It can be expressed roughly:

while (M ≠ N)
   subtract the smaller of M and N from the other
repeat until they are equal.

```
      PROGRAM EUCLID
      WRITE(UNIT=*, FMT=*) 'Enter two integers'
      READ(UNIT=*, FMT=*) M, N
10    IF(M .NE. N) THEN
         IF(M .GT. N) THEN
            M = M - N
         ELSE
            N = N - M
         END IF
         GO TO 10
      END IF
      WRITE(UNIT=*, FMT=*) 'Highest common factor = ', M
      END
```

8.6 Computed GO TO Statement

The computed GO TO statement is an alternative to the block-IF when a large number of options are required and they can be selected by the value of an integer expression. The general form of the statement is:

   GO TO ($label_1$, $label_2$, ... $label_N$), $integer$-$expression$

The comma after the right parenthesis is optional.

The expression is evaluated; if its value is one then control is transferred to the statement attached to the first label in the list; if it is two control goes to the second label, and so on. If the value of the expression is less than one or higher than N (where there are N labels in the list) then the statement has no effect and execution continues with the next statement in sequence. The same label may be present more than once in the list.

The computed GO TO suffers from many of the same drawbacks as the unconditional GO TO, since if its branches are used without restraint they can become impenetrable thickets. The best way is to follow the computed GO TO statement with the sections of code in order, all except the last terminated with its own unconditional GO TO to transfer control to the end of the whole structure.

Any computed GO TO structure could be replaced by an IF-block with a suitable number of ELSE IF clauses. If there is a very large number of cases then this would be a little less efficient; this has to be balanced against the increased clarity of the IF structure compared to the label-ridden GO TO.

An example of the use of the computed GO TO is given here in a subroutine which computes the number of days in a month, given the month number MONTH between 1 and 12, and the four-digit year number in YEAR. Note that each section of code except the last is terminated with a GO TO statement to escape from the structure.

```
      SUBROUTINE CALEND(YEAR, MONTH, DAYS)
      INTEGER YEAR, MONTH, DAYS
      GO TO (310, 280, 310, 300, 310, 300,
*            Jan  Feb  Mar  Apr  May  Jun
     $       310, 310, 300, 310, 300, 310) MONTH
*            Jly  Aug  Sep  Oct  Nov  Dec
      STOP 'Impossible month number'
*February: has 29 days in leap year, 28 otherwise.
280   IF(MOD(YEAR,400).EQ.0 .OR. (MOD(YEAR,100) .NE. 0
     $    .AND. MOD(YEAR,4) .EQ. 0)) THEN
         DAYS = 29
      ELSE
         DAYS = 28
      END IF
      GO TO 1000
*     Short months
300   DAYS = 30
      GO TO 1000
*     Long months
310   DAYS = 31
* return the value of DAYS
1000  END
```

8.7 Stop Statement

The STOP statement simply terminates the execution of the program and returns control to the operating system. Its general form is:

STOP 'character constant'

The character string (which must be a literal and not a named constant) is optional: if present its value is 'made available' to the user; usually the message appears on your terminal. For compatibility with Fortran 66 it is possible to use a string of one to five decimal digits instead of the character constant.

Ideally a program should only return control to the operating system from one point, the end of the main program, where the END statement does all that is necessary. In practice, even in the best-planned programs, situations can arise which make it pointless to continue. If these are detected in the main program there is always the option of jumping to the END statement, but within procedures there may be no choice but to use a STOP statement.

9 Procedures

Any set of computations can be encapsulated in a procedure. The main purpose of a procedure is to allow the same set of operations to be invoked at different points in a program. Procedures also make it possible to use the same code in several different programs. It is good practice to split a large program into sections whenever it becomes too large to be handled conveniently in one piece. The optimum size of a program unit is quite small, probably no more than 100 lines.

Four different forms of procedure can be used in Fortran programs:

- Intrinsic functions
- Statement functions
- External functions (also known as function subprograms)
- Subroutines.

Intrinsic functions are provided automatically by the Fortran system, whereas the other three forms of procedure are user-written. Statement functions, which are defined with the *statement function statement*, can be only be used in the program unit in which they were defined and are subject to other special restrictions. External functions and subroutines are two alternative forms of *external procedure*: each is specified as a separate program unit and can be used (with only a few restrictions) anywhere else in the program.

9.1 Intrinsic Functions

Intrinsic functions have a number of unique properties. The data type of each intrinsic function is known to the Fortran system and is not subject to the normal rules. IMPLICIT and *type* statements alone have no effect on them. Some intrinsic functions have *generic* names: when these are used the compiler selects the appropriate specific function according to the data type of the arguments.

A few intrinsic functions such as MAX, MIN and CMPLX, are allowed to have a variable number of arguments, but all of the arguments must have the same data type. User-written procedures cannot have optional arguments or generic type.

Although intrinsic functions can be used in any program unit, their names are not global, nor are they reserved words. It is, however, best to avoid choosing for a variable or array a name which is identical to that of an intrinsic function. It may cause confusion and in the long run it may make it more difficult to enhance the program. A name clash is more serious if it involves an external function or subroutine, for in this case the external procedure name must be specified in an EXTERNAL statement to resolve the ambiguity. By this means it is possible to substitute an external function of your own for one of the intrinsic functions.

The Fortran Standard specifies a fairly extensive set of intrinsic functions which must always be available but it does not prevent the provision of additional ones. Many systems provide additional intrinsic functions which, for example, obtain the current date and time, generate pseudo-random numbers, or evaluate Gaussian probability. The main drawback in using non-standard functions is that you may have to find a substitute if your program is moved to another system which does not have the same extensions.

The standard intrinsic functions for the arithmetic types are described in detail in section 6.2; those used with character-strings are covered in section 7.5. A complete alphabetical list is provided in Appendix C.

9.2 Statement Functions

Statement functions can be defined within any executable program unit by means of *statement function statements*. They can only be used, however, within the same program unit. Although statement functions have limited uses, they are unjustly neglected by many programmers.

The *statement function statement* resembles an ordinary assignment statement. For example:

```
FAHR(CELS) = 32.0 + 1.8 * CELS
```

The function FAHR converts a temperature in degrees Celsius to its equivalent in Fahrenheit. Thus FAHR(20.0) would return a value 68.0 approximately.

A statement function can have any number of *dummy arguments* (such as CELS above) all of which must appear in the expression on the right-hand side; this expression may also include constants, variables, or array elements used elsewhere in the program. When the function is called the current values of these items will be used. For example:

```
REAL M1, M2, G, R
NEWTON(M1, M2, R) = G * M1 * M2 / R**2
```

A reference to the function in an assignment statement such as:

```
FORCE = NEWTON(X, Y, DIST)
```

will return a value depending on the values of the actual arguments X, Y and DIST, and that of the variable G at the time the function is referenced.

Definitions of statement functions can also include references to intrinsic functions, external functions, or previously defined statement functions:

```
PARAMETER (PI = 3.14159265, DTOR = PI/180.0)
SIND(THETA) = SIN (THETA * DTOR)
COSD(THETA) = COS (THETA * DTOR)
TAND(THETA) = SIND(THETA) / COSD(THETA)
```

These definitions allow trigonometry on angles specified in degrees rather than radians.

The scope of each dummy argument name (such as THETA above) is that of the statement alone; these names can be used elsewhere in the program unit as variables of the same data type with no effect whatever on the evaluation of the function.

Statement functions can have any data type; the name and arguments follow the normal type rules. They can be useful in character handling, for example:

```
LOGICAL MATH, DIGIT, DORM
CHARACTER C*1
DIGIT(C) = LGE(C, '0') .AND. LLE(C, '9')
MATH (C) = INDEX('+-*/', C) .NE. 0
DORM (C) = DIGIT(C) .OR. MATH(C)
```

These three functions each return a logical value when presented with a single character argument: DIGIT tests to see whether the character is a digit, MATH tests whether it is an operator symbol, and DORM will test for either condition. Note the use of the lexical comparison functions LGE and LLE in the definition of DIGIT which make it completely independent of the local character code.

Statement function rules

Statement function statements must appear after any of the specification statements but before all executable statements in the program unit. They may be intermixed with DATA and FORMAT statements. The general form is:

   function (*dummy*$_1$, *dummy*$_2$, ... *dummy*$_n$) = *expression*

The function may have any data type; the expression will normally have the same data type but if both have an arithmetic type then the normal conversion rules for arithmetic assignment statements apply.

The *name* of the function must be distinct from all other symbolic names in the program unit. It may appear in *type* statements but not in other specification statements. (There is one exception: a common block is permitted to have the same name as a statement function but since common block names always appear between slashes there is little risk of confusion.) If the function has character type its length must be an integer constant expression.

The dummy arguments are simply symbolic names. A name may not appear more than once in the same list. These names may be used elsewhere in the program unit as variables of the same data type.

The *expression* must contain the dummy arguments as operands. The operands may also include:

- Literal constants, named constants, variables, and array elements; these will have their values at the time the function is executed and must then be defined.
- References to intrinsic and external functions.
- References to statement functions defined earlier in the same program unit.
- Complete expressions enclosed in parentheses.

Note that character substrings are not permitted. The variables and array elements used in the expression must be defined at the time that the function reference is executed.

Guidelines

Although statement functions have a limited role to play in programs because they can only be defined in a single statement, references to statement functions may be executed more efficiently than references to external functions; many modern compilers expand statement function references to in-line code when it is advantageous to do so.

If the same statement function is needed in more than one program unit it is possible to use an INCLUDE facility to provide the same definition each time, but it will usually be better to use an external function instead.

9.3 External Procedures

There are two forms of external procedure, both of which take the form of a complete program unit.
- External functions, which are specified by a program unit starting with a FUNCTION statement. They are executed whenever the corresponding function is used as an operand in an expression.
- Subroutines, which are specified by a program unit starting with a SUBROUTINE statement. They are executed in response to a CALL statement.

In either form the last statement of the program unit must be an END statement. Any other statements (except PROGRAM or BLOCK DATA statements) may be used within the program unit.

There are two statements provided especially for use in external procedures. The SAVE statement ensures that the values of local variables and arrays are preserved after the procedure returns control to the calling unit: these values will then be available if the procedure is executed subsequently. The RETURN statement may be used to terminate the execution of the procedure and cause an immediate return to the control of the calling unit. Execution of the END statement at the end of the procedure has exactly the same effect. Both of these are described in full later in the chapter.

Most Fortran systems also allow external procedures to be specified in languages other than Fortran: they can be called in the same way as Fortran procedures but their internal operations are, of course, beyond the scope of this book.

It is best to think of the subroutine as the more general form of procedure; the external function should be regarded as a special case for use when you only need to return a single value to the calling unit.

Here is a simple example of a procedure which converts a time of day in hours, minutes and seconds into a count of seconds since midnight. Since only one value needs to be returned, the procedure can have the form of an external function. (In fact this is such a simple example that it would have been possible to define it as a statement function.)

```
*TSECS converts hours, minutes, seconds to total seconds.
      REAL FUNCTION TSECS(NHOURS, MINS, SECS)
      INTEGER NHOURS, MINS
      REAL SECS
      TIME = ((NHOURS * 60) + MINS) * 60 + SECS
      END
```

Thus if we use a function reference like TSECS(12,30,0.0) in an expression elsewhere in the program it will convert the time to seconds since midnight (about 45000.0 seconds in this case). The items in parentheses after the function name

    (12,30,0.0)

are known as the *actual arguments* of the function; these values are transferred to the corresponding *dummy arguments*

    (NHOURS, MINS, SECS)

of the procedure before it is executed. In this example the argument list is used only to transfer information into the function from outside, the function name itself returns the required value to the calling program. In subroutines, however, there is no function name to return information but the arguments can be used for transfers in either direction, or both. The rules permit them to be used in this more general way in functions, but it is a practice best avoided.

The next example performs the inverse conversion to the TSECS function. Since it has to return three values to the calling program unit the functional form is no longer appropriate, and a subroutine will be used instead.

```
*Subroutine HMS converts TIME in seconds into hours, mins,
*secs
      SUBROUTINE HMS(TIME, NHOURS, MINS, SECS)
      REAL TIME, SECS
      INTEGER NHOURS, MINS
      NHOURS = INT(TIME / 3600.0)
      SECS   = TIME - 3600.0 * NHOURS
      MINS   = INT(SECS / 60.0)
      SECS   = TIME - 60.0 * MINS
      END
```

In this case the subroutine could be executed by using a statement such as:

```
      CALL HMS(45000.0, NHRS, MINS, SECS)
      WRITE(UNIT=*, FMT=*) NHRS, MINS, SECS
```

Here the first argument transfers information into the subroutine, the other three are used to return the values which it calculates. You do not have to specify whether a particular argument is to transfer information in or out (or in both directions), but there are rules about the form of actual argument that you can use in each case. These are explained in full below.

Procedure independence

Each program unit has its own independent set of symbolic names and labels. Type statements and IMPLICIT statements may be used to specify their data types.

External procedures can themselves call any other procedures and these may call others in turn, but procedures are not allowed to call themselves either directly or indirectly; that is, *recursive* calling is not permitted in Fortran.

Information transfer

Information can be transferred to and from an external procedure by any of three methods.

(1) An argument list: as shown in the two examples above. This is the preferred method of interfacing as it is the most flexible and modular. It is described in detail in the remainder of this chapter.

(2) Common blocks: these are lists of variables or arrays which are stored in areas of memory shared between two or more program units. They are useful in special circumstances when procedures have to be coupled closely together, but are otherwise less satisfactory. Common blocks are covered in detail in chapter 12.

(3) External files: interfacing via external files is neither convenient nor efficient but it is mentioned here to point out that external files are global. Once a file has been opened in any program unit it can be accessed anywhere in the program provided that the appropriate I/O unit number is available. A unit number can be passed into a procedure as an integer argument.

Procedure execution

It is not necessary to know how the Fortran system actually transfers information from one procedure to another to make use of the system, but the rules governing the process are somewhat complicated and it may be easier to understand them if you appreciate the basis on which they have been formulated. The rules in the Fortran Standard are based on the assumption that the *address* of an actual argument is transferred in each case: this may or may not be true in practice but the properties will be the same as if it is.

This means that when you reference a dummy variable or assign a new value to one, you are likely to be using the memory location occupied by the actual argument. By this means even large arrays can be transferred efficiently to procedures. A slight modification of this system is needed for items of character type so that the length of the item can be transferred as well as its address.

When a function reference or CALL statement is executed any expressions in the argument list are evaluated; the addresses of the arguments are then passed to the procedure. When it returns control this automatically makes updated values available to the corresponding items in the actual argument list.

Functions with side-effects

The rules of Fortran allow functions to have side-effects; that is, to alter their actual arguments or to change other variables within common blocks. Functions with side-effects cannot be used in expressions where any of the other operands of the expression would be affected, nor can they be used in subscript or substring references when any other expression used in the same references would be affected. This rule ensures that the value of an expression cannot depend arbitrarily on the way in which the computer chooses to evaluate it.

There are also restrictions on functions which make use of input/output statements even on internal files: these cannot be used in expressions in other I/O statements. This is to avoid the I/O system being used recursively.

By far the best course is to use the subroutine form for any procedure with side-effects.

9.4 Arguments of External Procedures

Arguments can pass information into a procedure or out from it, or in both directions. This just depends on the way that the dummy argument is used within the procedure. Although any argument order is permitted, it is common practice to put input arguments first, then those that pass information both ways, and then arguments which just return information from the procedure.

The rules for argument association are the same for both forms of external procedure. The list of *dummy arguments* (sometimes called formal arguments) of an external procedure is specified in its FUNCTION or SUBROUTINE statement. There can be any number of arguments, including none at all. If there are no arguments then the parentheses can be omitted in the CALL and SUBROUTINE statement but not in a FUNCTION statement or function reference.

The dummy argument list is simply a list of symbolic names which can represent any mixture of

- Variables
- Arrays
- Procedures.

A name cannot, of course, appear twice in the same dummy argument list.

Dummy variables, arrays and procedures are distinguished only by the way that they are used within the procedure. The dimension bounds of a dummy array must be specified in a subsequent type or DIMENSION statement; dummy procedures must appear in a CALL or EXTERNAL statement or be used in a function reference; anything else is, by elimination, a dummy argument variable.

Dummy argument variables and arrays can be used in executable statements in just the same way as local items of the same form, but they cannot appear in SAVE, COMMON, DATA or EQUIVALENCE statements.

Argument association

The actual arguments of the function reference or CALL statement become *associated* with the corresponding dummy arguments of the FUNCTION or SUBROUTINE statement. The main rules are as follows:

- There must be the same number of actual and dummy arguments; they are associated solely by their position in the two lists. Optional arguments are not permitted in Fortran 77.

- If the dummy argument is a variable, array or procedure used as a function, then the corresponding actual argument must have the same data type.

- If the dummy argument is an array then its array bounds must not be larger than those of the corresponding actual argument. Alternatively the dimension bounds of a dummy array can be passed in by means of other procedure arguments to form an *adjustable* array. This option and the *assumed-size* array are both described in section 9.6.

- If the dummy argument is a character item then its length must not be greater than that of the corresponding actual argument. Alternatively there is a passed-length option for character arguments: see section 9.5.

Because program units are compiled independently, it is difficult for the compiler to check for mismatches in actual and dummy argument lists. Although mismatches could, in principle, be detected by the linker, this rarely seems to happen in practice. Errors, particularly mismatches of data type or array bounds, are especially easy to make but hard to detect. Sometimes the only indication is that the program produces the wrong answer. This shows how important it is to check procedure interfaces.

Duplicate arguments

The same actual argument cannot be used more than once in a procedure call if the corresponding dummy arguments are assigned new values. For example, with:

```
SUBROUTINE FUNNY(X, Y)
X = 2.0
Y = 3.0
END
```

A call such as:

```
CALL FUNNY(A, A)
```

would be illegal because the system would try to assign both 2.0 and 3.0 to the variable A.

A similar restriction applies to variables which are returned via a common block and also through the procedure argument list.

9.5 Variables as Dummy Arguments

If the dummy argument of a procedure is a variable and it has a value assigned to it within the procedure, then the corresponding actual argument can be:

- a variable,
- an array element, or
- a character substring.

If, however, the dummy variable preserves its initial value throughout the execution then the actual argument can be any of these three forms above or alternatively:

- an expression of any form (including a constant).

The reason for these restrictions is easy to see by considering the ways of calling the subroutine SILLY in the next example:

```
SUBROUTINE SILLY(N, M)
N = N + M
END
```

If it is called with a statement such as:

```
NUMBER = 10
CALL SILLY(NUMBER, 5)
```

then the value of NUMBER will be updated to 15 as a result of the call. But it is illegal to call the function with a constant as the first argument, thus:

```
CALL SILLY(10, 7)
```

because on exit the subroutine will attempt to return the value of 17 to the actual argument which was specified as the constant ten. The effects of committing such an error are system-dependent. Some systems detect the attempt to over-write a constant and issue an error message; others ignore the attempt and allow the program to continue; but some systems will actually go ahead and over-write the constant with a new value, so that if you use the constant 10 in some subsequent statement in the program you may get a value of 17. Since this can have very puzzling effects and be hard to diagnose, it is important to avoid doing this inadvertently.

If you make use of procedures written by other people you may be worried about unintentional effects of this sort. In principle it should be possible to prevent a procedure altering a constant argument by turning each one into an expression, for example like this:

```
CALL SILLY(+10, +5)
```

or

```
CALL SILLY((10), (5))
```

Although either of these forms should protect the constants, it is still against the rules of Fortran for the procedure to attempt to alter the values of the corresponding dummy arguments. You will have to judge whether it is better to break the rules of the language than to risk corrupting a constant.

Expressions, subscripts and substrings

If the actual argument contains expressions then these are evaluated before the procedure starts to execute; even if the procedure later modifies operands of the expression this has no effect on the value passed to the dummy argument. The same rule applies to array subscript and character substring expressions. For example, if the procedure call consists of:

```
CALL SUB( ARRAY(N), N, SIN(4.0*N), TEXT(1:N) )
```

and the procedure assigns a new value to the second argument, N, during its execution, it has no effect on the other arguments which all use the original value of N. The updated value of N will, of course, be passed back to the calling unit.

Passed-length character arguments

A character dummy argument will have its length set automatically to that of the corresponding actual argument if the special length specification of*(*) is used.

To illustrate this, here is a procedure to count the number of vowels in a character string. It uses the intrinsic function LEN to determine the length of its dummy argument, and the INDEX function to see whether each character in turn is in the set 'AEIOU' or not.

```
      INTEGER FUNCTION VOWELS(STRING)
      CHARACTER*(*) STRING
      VOWELS = 0
      DO 25, K = 1,LEN(STRING)
         IF(INDEX('AEIOU', STRING(K:K)) .NE. 0) THEN
            VOWELS = VOWELS + 1
         END IF
25    CONTINUE
      END
```

Note that the function has a data type which is not the default for its initial letter so that it will usually be necessary to specify its name in a INTEGER statement in each program unit which references the function.

This passed-length mechanism is recommended not only for general-purpose software where the actual argument lengths are unknown, but in all cases unless there is a good reason to specify a dummy argument of fixed length.

There is one restriction on dummy arguments with passed length: they cannot be operands of the concatenation operator (//) except in assignment statements. Note that the same form of length specification '*(*)' can be used for named character constants but with a completely different meaning: named constants are not subject to this concatenation restriction.

9.6 Arrays as Arguments

If the dummy argument of a procedure is an array then the actual argument can be either:

- an array name (without subscripts)
- an array element.

The first form transfers the entire array; the second form, which just transfers a section starting at the specified element, is described in more detail further on.

The simplest, and most common, requirement is to make the entire contents of an array available in a procedure. If the actual argument arrays are always going to be the same size then the dummy arrays in the procedure can use fixed bounds. For example:

```
      SUBROUTINE DOT(X, Y, Z)
*Computes the dot product of arrays X and Y of 100 elements
*producing array Z of the same size.
      REAL X(100), Y(100), Z(100)
      DO 15, I = 1,100
         Z(I) = X(I) * Y(I)
15    CONTINUE
      END
```

This procedure could be used within a program unit like this:

```
      PROGRAM PROD
      REAL A(100), B(100), C(100)
      READ(UNIT=*,FMT=*)A,B
      CALL DOT(A, B, C)
      WRITE(UNIT=*,FMT=*)C
      END
```

This is perfectly legitimate, if inflexible, since it will not work on arrays of any other size.

Adjustable dummy arrays

A more satisfactory solution is to generalise the procedure so that it can be used on arrays of any size. This is done by using an *adjustable array* declaration. Here the operands in each dimension bound expression may include integer variables which are also arguments of the procedure (or members of a common block). The following example shows how this may be done:

```
      SUBROUTINE DOTPRO(NPTS, X, Y, Z)
      REAL X(NPTS), Y(NPTS), Z(NPTS)
      DO 15, I = 1, NPTS
* etc.
```

In this case the calling sequence would be something like:

```
CALL DOTPRO(100, A, B, C)
```

An adjustable array declaration is permitted only for arrays which are dummy arguments, since the actual array space has in this case already been allocated in the calling unit or at some higher level. The method can be extended in the obvious way to cover multi-dimensional arrays and those with upper and lower bounds, for example:

```
SUBROUTINE MULTI(MAP, K1, L1, K2, L2, TRACE)
DOUBLE PRECISION MAP(K1:L1, K2:L2)
REAL TRACE(L1-K1+1)
```

The adjustable array mechanism can, of course, be used for arrays of any data type; an adjustable array can also be passed as an actual argument of a procedure with, if necessary, the array bounds passed on in parallel.

Each array bound of a dummy argument array may be an integer expression involving not only constants but also integer variables passed in to the procedure either as arguments or by means of a common block. The extent of each dimension of the array must not be less than one and must not be greater than the extent of the corresponding dimension of the actual argument array.

If any integer variable (or named constant) used in an array-bound expression has a name which does not imply integer type then the INTEGER statement which specifies its type must precede its use in a dimension-bound expression.

Assumed-size dummy arrays

There may be circumstances in which it is impracticable to use either fixed or adjustable array declarations in a procedure because the actual size of the array is unknown when the procedure starts executing. In this case an assumed-size array is a viable alternative. These are also only permitted for dummy argument arrays of procedures, but here the array is, effectively, declared to be of unknown or indefinite size. For example:

```
REAL FUNCTION ADDTWO(TABLE, ANGLE)
REAL TABLE(*)
N = MAX(1, NINT(SIN(ANGLE) * 500.0))
ADDTWO = TABLE(N) + TABLE(N+1)
END
```

Here the procedure only knows that array TABLE is one-dimensional with a lower-bound of one: that is all it needs to know to access the appropriate elements N and N+1. In executing the procedure it is our responsibility to ensure that the value of ANGLE will never result in an array subscript which is out of range. This is always a danger with assumed-size arrays. Because the compiler does not have any information about the upper-bound of an assumed-size array it cannot use any array-bound checking code even if it is normally able to do this. An assumed-size array can only have the upper-bound of its last dimension specified by an asterisk, all the other bounds (if any) must conform to the normal rules (or be adjustable using integer arguments).

An assumed size dummy argument array is specified with an asterisk as the upper bound of its last (or only) dimension. All the other dimension bounds, if any, must conform to normal rules for local arrays or adjustable arrays.

There is one important restriction on assumed size arrays: they cannot be used without subscripts in I/O statements, for example in the input list of a READ statement or the output list of a WRITE statement. This is because the compiler has no information about the total size of the array when compiling the procedure.

Array sections

The rules of Fortran require that the extent of an array (in each dimension if it is multi-dimensional) must be at least as large in the actual argument as in the dummy argument, but they do not require actual agreement of both lower and upper bounds. For example:

```
PROGRAM CONFUS
REAL X(-1:50), Y(10:1000)
READ(UNIT=*,FMT=*) X, Y
CALL OUTPUT(X)
CALL OUTPUT(Y)
END

SUBROUTINE OUTPUT(ARRAY)
REAL ARRAY(50)
WRITE(UNIT=*,FMT=*) ARRAY
END
```

The effect of this program will be to output the elements X(-1) to X(48) since X(48) corresponds to ARRAY(50), and then output Y(10) to Y(59) also. The subroutine will work similarly on a slice through a two-dimensional array:

```
      PROGRAM TWODIM
      REAL D(100,20)
★ ...
      NSLICE = 15
      CALL OUTPUT(D(1,NSLICE))
```

In this example the slice of the array from elements D(1,15) to D(50,15) will be written to the output file. In order to work out what is going to happen you need to know that Fortran arrays are stored with the first subscript most rapidly varying, and that the argument association operates as if the address of the specified element were transferred to the base address of the dummy argument array.

The use of an array element as an actual argument when the dummy argument is a complete array is a very misleading notation and the transfer of array sections should be avoided if at all possible.

Character dummy arrays

When a dummy argument is a character array the passed-length mechanism can be used in the same way as for a character variable. Every element of the dummy array has the length that was passed in from the actual argument.

For example, a subroutine designed to sort an array of character strings into ascending order might start with specification statements like these:

```
      SUBROUTINE SORT(NELS, NAMES)
      INTEGER NELS
      CHARACTER NAMES(NELS)★(★)
```

The corresponding actual argument is usually a character array.

Alternatively the actual argument can be a character variable or substring. In such cases it usually makes more sense not to use the passed-length mechanism. For example an actual argument declared:

```
      CHARACTER★80 LINE
```

could be passed to a subroutine which declared it as an array of four 20-character elements:

```
      SUBROUTINE SPLIT(LINE)
      CHARACTER LINE(4)★20
```

Although this is valid Fortran, it is not a very satisfactory programming technique to use a procedure call to alter the shape of an item so radically.

9.7 Procedures as Arguments

Fortran allows one procedure to be used as the actual argument of another procedure. This provides a powerful facility, though one that most programmers use only rarely. Procedures are normally used to carry out a given set of operations on different sets of *data*; but sometimes you want to carry out the same set of operations on different *functional forms*. Examples include: finding the gradient of a function, integrating the area under a curve, or simply plotting a graph. If the curve is specified as a set of data points then you can simply pass over an array, but if it is specified by means of some algorithm then the procedure which evaluates it can itself be an actual argument.

In the next example, the subroutine GRAPH plots a graph of a function MYFUNC between specified limits, with its argument range divided somewhat arbitrarily into 101 points. For simplicity it assumes the existence of a subroutine PLOT which moves the pen to position (X,Y). Some other subroutines would, in practice, almost certainly be required.

```
      SUBROUTINE GRAPH(MYFUNC, XMIN, XMAX)
*Plots functional form of MYFUNC(X) with X in range
*XMIN:XMAX.
      REAL MYFUNC, XMIN, XMAX
      XDELTA = (XMAX - XMIN) / 100.0
      DO 25, I = 0,100
           X = XMIN + I * XDELTA
           Y = MYFUNC(X)
           CALL PLOT(X, Y)
25    CONTINUE
      END
```

The procedure GRAPH can then be used to plot a function simply by providing its name as the first argument of the call. The only other requirement is that the name of each function used as an actual argument in this way must be specified in an INTRINSIC or EXTERNAL statement, as appropriate. Thus:

```
      PROGRAM CURVES
      INTRINSIC SIN, TAN
      EXTERNAL MESSY
      CALL GRAPH(SIN, 0.0, 3.14159)
      CALL GRAPH(TAN, 0.0, 0.5)
      CALL GRAPH(MESSY, 0.1, 0.9)
      END

      REAL FUNCTION MESSY(X)
      PRETTY = COS(0.1*X) + 0.02 * SIN(SQRT(X))
      END
```

This will first plot a graph of the sine function, then of the tangent function with a different range, and finally produce another plot of the external function called MESSY. These functions must, of course, have the same procedure interface themselves and must be called correctly in the GRAPH procedure.

It is possible to pass either a function or a subroutine as an actual argument in this way: the only difference is that a CALL statement is used instead of a function reference to execute the dummy procedure. It is possible to pass a procedure through more than one level of procedure call in the same way. Continuing the last example, another level could be introduced like this:

```
PROGRAM CURVE2
EXTERNAL MESSY
INTRINSIC SIN, TAN
CALL GRAPH2(PRETTY)
CALL GRAPH2(TAN)
END

SUBROUTINE GRAPH2(PROC)
EXTERNAL PROC
CALL GRAPH(PROC, 0.1, 0.7)
END
```

Thus the procedure GRAPH2 sets limits to each plot and passes the procedure name on to GRAPH. The symbolic name PROC must be declared in an EXTERNAL statement as it is a *dummy procedure*: an EXTERNAL statement is required whether the actual procedure at the top level is intrinsic or external. The syntax of the INTRINSIC and EXTERNAL statements is given in section 9.12.

The name of an intrinsic function used as an actual argument must be a *specific* name and not a *generic* one. This is the only circumstance in which you still have to use specific names for intrinsic functions. A full list of specific names is given in Appendix C. A few of the most basic intrinsic functions are often expanded to in-line code (those for type conversion, lexical comparison, as well as MIN and MAX) and cannot be passed as actual arguments.

9.8 SUBROUTINE and CALL Statements

It is convenient to describe these two statements together as they have to be closely matched in use. The general form of the SUBROUTINE statement is:

SUBROUTINE *name* (*dummy*$_1$, *dummy*$_2$, ... *dummy*$_N$)

or

SUBROUTINE *name*

The second form just indicates that if there are no arguments then the parentheses are optional.

The symbolic name of the subroutine becomes a global name; it must not be used at all within the program unit and must not be used for any other global item within the entire executable program.

The dummy arguments are also simply symbolic names. The way in which these are interpreted is covered in the next section.

The CALL statement has a similar general form:

    CALL name (arg_1, arg_2, ... arg_N)

or:

    CALL name

Again, if there are no arguments the parentheses are optional.

The *name* must be that of a subroutine (or dummy subroutine). Each *arg* is an actual argument which can be a variable, array, substring, array element or any form of expression. The permitted forms, which depend on the form of the corresponding dummy argument and how it is used within the subroutine, are fully described in the preceding sections.

9.9 RETURN Statement

The RETURN statement just consists of the keyword

    RETURN

Its effect is to stop the procedure executing and to return control, and where appropriate argument and function values, to the calling program unit. The execution of the END statement at the end of the program unit has exactly the same effect, so that RETURN is superfluous in procedures which have only one entry and one exit point (as all well-designed procedures should). It is, however, sometimes convenient to use RETURN for an emergency exit. Here is a simple example to illustrate the point:

```
      REAL FUNCTION HYPOT(X, Y)
*Computes the hypotenuse of a right-angled triangle.
      REAL X, Y
      IF(X .LE. 0.0 .OR. Y .LE. 0.0) THEN
          WRITE(UNIT=*,FMT=*)'impossible triangle'
          HYPOT = 0.0
          RETURN
      END IF
      HYPOT = SQRT(X**2 + Y**2)
      END
```

This function could be used in another program unit like this:

```
X = HYPOT(12.0, 5.0)
Y = HYPOT(0.0, 5.0)
```

which would assign to X the value of 13.0000 approximately, while the second function call would cause a warning message to be issued and would return a value of zero to Y.

In the external function shown above it would have been perfectly possible to avoid having two exit points by an alternative ending to the procedure, such as:

```
IF(X .LE. 0.0 .OR. Y .LE. 0.0) THEN
    WRITE(UNIT=*,FMT=*)'Warning: impossible
 $  values'
    HYPOT = 0.0
ELSE
    HYPOT = SQRT(X**2 + Y**2)
END IF
END
```

In more realistic cases, however, the main part of the calculation would be much longer than just one statement and it might then be easier to understand the working if a RETURN statement were to be used than with almost all of the procedure contained within an ELSE-block. A third possibility for emergency exits is to use an unconditional GO TO statement to jump to a label placed on the END statement.

9.10 FUNCTION Statement

The FUNCTION statement must be the first statement of every external function. Its general form is:

$$\textit{type}\ \text{FUNCTION}(\ \textit{dummy}_1,\ \textit{dummy}_2,\ \ldots\ \textit{dummy}_N)$$

The *type* specification is optional: if it is omitted then the type of the result is determined by the usual rules. The function name may have its type specified by a *type* or IMPLICIT statement which appears later in the program unit. If the function is of type character then the length may be specified by a literal constant (but not a named constant) or may be given in the form CHARACTER*(*) in which case the length will be passed in as the length declared for the function name in the calling program unit.

There may be any number of dummy arguments including none, but the parentheses must still be present. Dummy arguments may, as described in section 9.4, be variables, arrays or procedures.

The function name may be used as a variable within the function subprogram unit; a value *must* be assigned to this variable before the procedure returns control to the calling unit. If the function name used the passed-length option then the corresponding variable cannot be used as an operand of the concatenation operator except in an assignment statement. The passed-length option is less useful for character functions than for arguments because the length is inevitably the same for all references from the same program unit. For example:

```
      PROGRAM FLEX
      CHARACTER CODE*8, CLASS*6, TITLE*16
      CLASS = CODE('SECRET')
      TITLE = CODE('ORDER OF BATTLE')
      END

      CHARACTER*(*) FUNCTION CODE(WORD)
      CHARACTER WORD*(*), BUFFER*80
      DO 15, K = 1,LEN(WORD)
          BUFFER(K:K) = CHAR(ICHAR(WORD(K:K) + 1)
15    CONTINUE
      CODE = BUFFER
      END
```

Unfortunately, although this function can take in an argument of any length up to 80 characters long and encode it, it can only return a result of exactly 8 characters long when called from the program FLEX, so that it will not produce the desired result when provided with the longer character string. This limitation could be overcome with the use of a subroutine with a second passed-length argument to handle the returned value. Functions without arguments do not have a wide range of uses but applications for them do occur from time to time, for example when generating random numbers or reading values from an input file. For example:

```
      PROGRAM COPY
      REAL NEXT
      DO 10, I = 1,100
          WRITE(UNIT=*,FMT=*) NEXT()
10    CONTINUE
      END

      REAL FUNCTION NEXT()
      READ(UNIT=*,FMT=*) NEXT
      END
```

The parentheses are needed on the function call to distinguish it from a variable. The function statement itself also has to have the empty pair of parentheses, presumably to match the call.

9.11 SAVE Statement

SAVE is a specification statement which can be used to ensure that variables and arrays used within a procedure preserve their values between successive calls to the procedure. Under normal circumstances local items will become 'undefined' as soon as the procedure returns control to the calling unit. It is often useful to store the values of certain items used on one call to avoid doing extra work on the next. For example:

```
SUBROUTINE EXTRA(MILES)
INTEGER MILES, LAST
SAVE LAST
DATA LAST /0/
WRITE(UNIT=*, FMT=*) MILES - LAST, 'more miles.'
LAST = MILES
END
```

This subroutine simply saves the value of the argument MILES each time and subtracts it from the next one, so that it can print out the incremental value. The value of LAST had to be given an initial value using a DATA statement in order to prevent its use with an undefined value on the initial call.

Local variables and arrays and complete named common blocks can be saved using SAVE statements, but not variables and arrays which are dummy arguments or which appear within common blocks.

Items which are initially defined with a DATA statement but which are never updated with a new value do not need to be saved.

The SAVE statement has two alternative forms:

```
SAVE item, item, ... item
```

or

```
SAVE
```

Where each item can be a local variable or (unsubscripted) array, or the name of a common block enclosed in slashes. The second form, with no list of items, saves all the allowable items in the program unit. This form should not be used in any program unit which uses a common block unless all common blocks used in that program unit are also used in the main program or saved in every program unit in which it appears. The SAVE statement can be used in the main program unit (so that it could be packaged with other specifications in an INCLUDE file) but has no effect.

Many current Fortran systems have a simple static storage allocation scheme in which all variables are saved whether SAVE is used or not.

But on small computers which make use of disk overlays, or large ones with virtual memory systems, this may not be so. You should always take care to use the SAVE statement anywhere that its use is indicated to make your programs safe and portable. Even where it is at present strictly redundant it still indicates to the reader that the procedure works by retaining information from one call to the next, and this is valuable in itself.

9.12 EXTERNAL and INTRINSIC Statements

The EXTERNAL statement is used to name external procedures which are required in order to run a given program unit. It may specify the name of any external function or subroutine. It is required in three rather different circumstances:
- Whenever an external procedure or dummy procedure is used as the actual argument of another procedure call.
- To call any procedure which has a name duplicating an intrinsic function.
- To ensure that a named block data subprogram is linked into the complete executable program. This specialised use is covered further in section 12.4.

The INTRINSIC statement is used to declare a name to be that of an intrinsic function. It is normally necessary only when that function is to be used as the actual argument of another procedure call, but may also be advisable when calling a non-standard intrinsic function to remove any ambiguity which might arise if an external function of the same name also existed.

The general form of the two statements is the same,

```
EXTERNAL ename, ename, ... ename
```

and

```
INTRINSIC iname, iname, ... iname
```

Where *ename* can be the name of an external function or subroutine or a dummy procedure; *iname* must be the *specific* name of an intrinsic function. For example, to use the real and double precision versions of the trigonometric functions as actual arguments we need:

```
INTRINSIC SIN, COS, TAN, DCOS, DSIN, DTAN
```

When the function name SIN is used as an actual argument it refers to the specific *real* sine function; in other contexts it still has its usual generic property.

The use of procedures as actual arguments is covered in detail in section 9.7; a list of specific names of intrinsic functions is given in Appendix C.

10 Input/Output Facilities

The I/O system of Fortran is relatively powerful, flexible and well-defined. Programs can be portable and device-independent even if they make extensive use of input/output facilities: this is difficult if not impossible in many other high-level languages. The effects of the hardware and operating system cannot, of course, be ignored entirely but they usually only affect fairly minor matters such as the forms of file-name and the maximum record length that can be used.

The READ and WRITE statements are most common and generally look like this:

```
READ(UNIT=*, FMT=*) NUMBER
WRITE(UNIT=13, ERR=999) NUMBER, ARRAY(1), ARRAY(N)
```

The pair of parentheses after the word READ or WRITE encloses the *control-list*: a list of items which specifies where and how the data transfer takes place. The items in this list are usually specified with keywords. The list of data items to be read or written follow the control-list.

Other input/output statements have a similar form except that they only have a control-list. There are the file-handling statements OPEN, CLOSE and INQUIRE, as well as the REWIND and BACKSPACE statements which alter the currently active position within a file.

Before covering these statements in detail, it is necessary to explain some of the concepts and terminology involved.

10.1 Files, I/O Units and Records

In Fortran the term file is used for anything that can be handled with a READ or WRITE statement: the term covers not just data files stored on disk or tape, but also peripheral devices such as printers or terminals. Strictly these should all be called *external files*, to distinguish them from *internal files*.

An internal file is nothing more than a character variable or array which is used as a temporary file while the program is running. Internal files can be used with READ and WRITE statements in order to process character information under the control of a format specification. They cannot be used by other I/O statements.

Before an external file can be used it must be connected to an *I/O unit*. I/O units are integers which may be chosen freely from zero up to a system-dependent limit (usually at least 99). Except in OPEN and INQUIRE statements, files can only be referred to via their unit numbers.

The OPEN statement connects a named file to a numbered unit. It usually specifies whether the file already exists or whether a new one is to be created, for example:

```
OPEN(UNIT=1, FILE='B:INPUT.DAT', STATUS='OLD')
OPEN(UNIT=9, FILE='PRINTOUT', STATUS='NEW')
```

For simplicity most of the examples in this chapter show an actual integer as the unit identifier, but it helps to make software more modular and adaptable if a named constant or a variable is used instead.

I/O units are a *global* resource. A file can be opened in any program unit; once it is open I/O operations can be performed on it in that unit or any provided that the same unit number is used. The unit number can be held in an integer variable and passed to procedure as an argument.

The connection between a file and a unit, once established, persists until:

- The program terminates normally (at a STOP statement or the END of the main program).
- Another OPEN statement connects a different file to the same unit.
- A CLOSE statement is executed on that unit.

Although all files are closed when the program exits, it is good practice to close them explicitly as soon as I/O operations on them are completed. If the program terminates abnormally, for example because an error occurs or it is aborted by the user, any files which are open, especially output files, may be left with incomplete or corrupted records.

The INQUIRE statement can be used to obtain information about the current properties of external files and I/O units. INQUIRE is particularly useful when writing library procedures which may have to run in a variety of different program environments. You can find out, for example, which unit numbers are free for use, or whether a particular file exists and if so what its characteristics are.

Records

A file consists of a sequence of records. In a text file a record corresponds to a line of text; in other cases a record has no physical basis, it is just a convenient collection of values chosen to suit the application. There is no need for a record to correspond to a disk sector or a tape block. READ and WRITE statements always start work at the beginning of a record and always transfer a whole number of records.

The rules of Fortran set no upper limit to the length of a record but, in practice, each operating system may do so. This may be different for different forms of record.

Formatted and unformatted records

External files come in two varieties according to whether their records are formatted or unformatted. *Formatted records* store data in character-coded form, i.e. as lines of text. This makes them suitable for a wide range of applications since, depending on their contents, they may be legible to humans as well as computers. The main complication for the programmer is that each WRITE or READ statement must specify how each value is to be converted from internal to external form or vice versa. This is usually done with a *format specification*.

Unformatted records store data in the internal code of the computer so that no format conversions are involved. This has several advantages for files of numbers, especially floating-point numbers. Unformatted data transfers are simpler to program, faster in execution, and free from rounding errors. Furthermore the resulting data files, sometimes called *binary files*, are usually much smaller. A *real* number would, for example, have to be turned into a string of 10 or even 15 characters to preserve its precision on a formatted record, but on an unformatted record a real number typically occupies only 4 bytes, i.e. the same as 4 characters. The drawback is that unformatted files are highly system-specific. They are usually illegible to humans and to other brands of computer and sometimes incompatible with files produced by other programming languages on the same machine. Unformatted files should only be used for information to be written and read by Fortran programs running on the same type of computer.

Sequential and direct access

All peripheral devices allow files to be processed sequentially: you start at the beginning of the file and work through each record in turn. One important advantage of sequential files is that different records can have different lengths; the minimum record length is zero but the maximum is system-dependent.

Sequential files behave as if there were a pointer attached to the file which always indicates the next record to be transferred. On devices such as terminals and printers you can only read or write in strict sequential order, but when a file is stored on disk or tape it is possible to use the REWIND statement to reset this pointer to the start of the file, allowing it to be read in again or re-written.

On suitable files the BACKSPACE statement can be used to move the pointer back by one record so that the last record can be read again or over-written. One unfortunate omission from the Fortran Standard is that the position of the record pointer is not defined when an existing sequential file is opened. Most Fortran systems behave sensibly and make sure that they start at the beginning of the file, but there are a few rogue systems around which make it advisable, in portable software, to use REWIND after the OPEN statement. Another problem is how to *append* new records to an existing sequential file. Some systems provide (as an extension) an 'append' option in the OPEN statement, but the best method using Standard Fortran is to open the file and read records one at a time until the end-of-file condition is encountered; then use BACKSPACE to move the pointer back and clear the *end-of-file* condition. New records can then be added in the usual way.

The alternative access method is *direct-access* which allows records to be read and written in any order. Most systems only permit this for files stored on random-access devices such as disks; it is sometimes also permitted on tapes. All records in a direct-access file must be the same length so that the system can compute the location of a record from its record number. The record length has to be chosen when the file is created and (on most systems) is then fixed for the life of the file. In Fortran, direct-access records are numbered from one upwards; each READ or WRITE statement specifies the record number at which the transfer starts.

Records may be written to a direct-access file in any order. Any record can be read provided that it exists, i.e. it has been written at some time since the file was created. Once a record has been written there is no way of deleting it, but its contents can be updated, i.e. replaced, at any time.

A few primitive operating systems require the maximum length of a direct-access file to be specified when the file is created; this is not necessary in systems which comply fully with the Fortran Standard.

10.2 External Files

Formatted and *unformatted* records cannot be mixed on the same file and on most systems files designed for *sequential access* are quite distinct from those created for *direct access*: thus there are four different types of external file. There is no special support in Standard Fortran for any other types of file such as indexed-sequential files or name-list files.

Formatted sequential files

These are often just called text files. Terminals and printers should always be treated as formatted sequential files. Data files of this type can be created in a variety of ways, for example by direct entry from the keyboard, or by using a text editor. Some Fortran systems do not allow records to be longer than a normal line of text, for example 132 characters.

Unless a text file is pre-connected it must be opened with an OPEN statement, but the FORM= and ACCESS= keywords (see section 10.13) are not needed as the default values are suitable:

```
OPEN(UNIT=4, FILE='REPORT', STATUS='NEW')
```

All data transfers must be carried out under format control. There are two options with files of this type: you can either provide your own *format specification* or use *list-directed* formatting.

The attraction of *list-directed* I/O is that the Fortran system does the work, providing simple data transfers with little programming effort. They are specified by having an asterisk as the format identifier:

```
WRITE(UNIT=*, FMT=*)'Enter velocity: '
READ(UNIT=*, FMT=*, END=999) SPEED
```

List-directed input is quite convenient when reading numbers from a terminal since it allows virtually 'free-format' data entry. It may also be useful when reading data files where the layout is not regular enough to be handled by a format specification. List-directed output is satisfactory when used just to output a character string (as in the example above), but it produces less pleasing results when used to output numerical values since you have no control over the positioning of items on the line, the field-width, or the number of decimal digits displayed. Thus:

```
WRITE(UNIT=LP, FMT=*) 'Box of',N,' costs £',PRICE
```

will produce a record something like this:

Box of   12 costs £   9.5000000

List-directed output is best avoided except to write simple messages and for diagnostic output during program development. The rules for list-directed formatting are covered in detail in section 10.10.

The alternative is to provide a *format specification*: this provides complete control over the data transfer. The previous example can be modified to use a format specification like this:

```
      WRITE(UNIT=LP, FMT=55)'Box of',N,' costs £',PRICE
55    FORMAT(1X, A, I3, A, F6.2)
```

and will produce a record like this:

Box of 12 costs £   9.50

The format specification is provided in this case by a FORMAT statement: its label is the format identifier in the WRITE statement. Other ways of providing format specifications are described in section 10.6.

One unusual feature of input under control of a format specification is that each line of text will appear to be padded out on the right with an indefinite number of blanks irrespective of the actual length of the data record. This means that, among other things, it is not possible to distinguish between an empty record and one filled with blanks. If numbers are read from an empty record they will simply be zero.

Unformatted sequential files

Unformatted sequential files are often used to transfer data from one program to another. They are also suitable for *scratch* files, i.e. those used temporarily during program execution. The only limit on the length of unformatted records is that set by the operating system; most systems allow records to contain a few thousand data items at least. The OPEN statement must specify the file format, but the default access method is 'sequential'. Each READ or WRITE statement transfers one unformatted record.

For example, these statements open an existing unformatted file and read two records from it:

```
      OPEN(UNIT=15, FILE='BIN', STATUS='OLD',
     $  FORM='UNFORMATTED')
      READ(15) HEIGHT, LENGTH, WIDTH
      READ(15) ARRAYP, ARRAYQ
```

BACKSPACE and REWIND statements may generally be used on all unformatted sequential files.

Unformatted direct-access files

Since direct-access files are readable only by machine, it seems sensible to use unformatted records to maximise efficiency. The OPEN statement must specify ACCESS='DIRECT' and also specify the record length. Unfortunately, the units used to measure the length of a record are not standardised: some systems measure them in bytes, others in *numerical storage units*, i.e. the number of real or integer variables a record can hold (see section 5.1). This is a minor obstacle to portability and means that you may need to know how many bytes your machine uses for each *numerical storage unit*, although this is just about the only place in Fortran where this is necessary. Most systems will allow you to open an existing file only if the record length is the same as that used when the file was created.

Each READ and WRITE statement transfers exactly one record and must specify the number of that record: an integer value from one upwards. The record length must not be greater than that declared in the OPEN statement; if an output record is not completely filled the remainder is undefined.

To illustrate how direct-access files can be used, here is a complete program which allows a very simple database, such as a set of stock records, to be examined. Assuming that the record length is measured in numerical storage units of 4 bytes, the required record length in this case can be computed as follows:

NAME	1	CHARACTER*10 variable	10 chars	=	10 bytes
STOCK	1	INTEGER variable	1 unit	=	4 bytes
PRICE	1	REAL variable	1 unit	=	4 bytes

The total record length is 18 bytes or 5 numerical storage units (rounding up to the next integer).

```
      PROGRAM DBASE1
      INTEGER STOCK, NERR
      REAL PRICE
      CHARACTER NAME*10
*Assume record length in storage units holding 4
*chars each.
      OPEN(UNIT=1, FILE='STOCKS', STATUS='OLD',
     $   ACCESS='DIRECT', RECL=5)
100   CONTINUE
*Ask user for part number which will be used as
*record number.
      WRITE(UNIT=*,FMT=*)
     $   'Enter part number (or zero to quit):'
      READ(UNIT=*,FMT=*) NPART
```

```
      IF(NPART .LE. 0) STOP
      READ(UNIT=1, REC=NPART, IOSTAT=NERR) NAME,
     $   STOCK, PRICE
      IF(NERR .NE. 0) THEN
          WRITE(UNIT=*,FMT=*) 'Unknown part, re-enter'
          GO TO 100
      END IF
      WRITE(*,115)STOCK, NAME, PRICE
115   FORMAT(1X,'Stock is',I4,1X,A,'at £',F8.2,'each')
      GO TO 100
      END
```

The typical output record of the program will be of the form:

'Stock is 123 widgets at £556.89 each'

This program could be extended fairly easily to allow the contents of the record to be updated as the stock changes.

Formatted direct-access files

Formatted direct-access files are slightly more portable than the unformatted form because their record length is always measured in characters. Otherwise there is little to be said for them. The OPEN statement must specify both ACCESS='DIRECT' and FORM='FORMATTED' and each READ and WRITE statement must contain both format and record-number identifiers. List-directed transfers are not permitted. If the format specification requires more than one record to be used, these additional records follow on sequentially from that specified by REC=. It is an error to try to read beyond the end of a record, but an incompletely filled record will be padded out with blanks.

10.3 Internal Files

An internal file is an area of central memory which can be used as if it were a formatted sequential file. It exists, of course, only while the program is executing. Internal files are used for a variety of purposes, particularly to carry out data conversions to and from *character* data type. Some earlier versions of Fortran included ENCODE and DECODE statements: the internal file READ (which replaces DECODE) and internal file WRITE (which replaces ENCODE) are simpler, more flexible, and entirely portable.

An internal file can only be used with READ and WRITE statements and an explicit format specification is required: list-directed transfers are not permitted. The *unit* must have character data type but it can be a variable, array element, substring, or a complete array. If it is a complete array then each array element constitutes a record; in all other cases the file only consists of one record. Data transfers always start at the beginning of the internal file; that is, an implicit rewind is performed each time. The record length is the length of the character item. It is illegal to try to transfer more characters than the internal file contains, but if a record of too few characters is written it will be padded out with blanks. The END= and IOSTAT= mechanisms can be used to detect the end-of-file.

An internal file WRITE is typically used to convert a numerical value to a character string by using a suitable format specification, for example:

```
CHARACTER*8 CVAL
RVALUE = 98.6
WRITE(CVAL, '(SP, F7.2)') RVALUE
```

The WRITE statement will fill the character variable CVAL with the characters ' +98.60 ' (note that there is one blank at each end of the number, the first because the number is right-justified in the field of 7 characters, the second because the record is padded out to the declared length of 8 characters).

Once a number has been turned into a character-string it can be processed further in the various ways described in Chapter 7. This makes it possible, for example, to write numbers left-justified in a field, or mark negative numbers with with 'DR' (as in bank statements) or even use a pair of parentheses (as in balance sheets). With suitable arithmetic you can even output values in other number bases such as octal or hexadecimal. Even more elaborate conversions may be achieved by first writing a suitable format specification into a character string and then using that format to carry out the desired conversion.

Internal file READ statements can be used to decode a character string containing a numerical value. One obvious application is to handle the user input to a command-driven program. Suppose the command line consists of a word followed, optionally, by a number (in integer or real format), with at least one blank separating the two. Thus the input commands might be something like:

```
UP 4
RIGHT 123.45
```

A simple way to deal with this is to read the whole line into a character variable and then use the INDEX function to locate the first blank. The preceding characters constitute the command word, those following can be converted to a real number using an internal file READ. For example:

```
          CHARACTER CLINE*80
*   .  .
100       WRITE(UNIT=*,FMT=*)'Enter command: '
          READ(UNIT=*, FMT='(A)' IOSTAT=KODE) CLINE
          IF(KODE .NE. 0) STOP
          K = INDEX(CLINE,' ')
*The command word is now in CLINE(1:K-1); Assume the
*number is in the next 20 characters: read it into
*RVALUE
          READ(UNIT=CLINE(K+1:), FMT= '(BN,F20.0)',
     $        IOSTAT=KODE) REVALUE
          IF(KODE .NE. 0) THEN
              WRITE(UNIT=*,FMT=*)'Error: try again'
              GO TO 100
          END IF
```

Note that the edit descriptor BN is needed to ensure that any trailing blanks will be ignored; the F20.0 will then handle any real or integer constant anywhere in the next 20 characters. A field of blanks will be converted into zero.

10.4 Pre-Connected Files

Terminal input/output

Many programs are interactive and need to access the user's terminal. Although the terminal is a file which can be connected with an OPEN statement, its name is system-dependent. Fortran solves the problem by providing two special files usually called the *standard input file* and the *standard output file*. These files are pre-connected, i.e. no OPEN statement is needed (or permitted). They are both *formatted sequential* files and, on interactive systems, handle input and output to the terminal. You can READ and WRITE from these files simply by having an asterisk '*' as the unit identifier. These files make terminal I/O simple and portable; examples of their use can be found throughout this book.

When a program is run in batch mode most systems arrange for standard output to be diverted to a log file or to the system printer. There may be some similar arrangement for the standard input file.

The asterisk notation has one slight drawback: the unit number is often specified by an integer variable so that the source of input or destination of output can be switched from one file to another merely be altering the value of this integer. This cannot be done with the standard input or output files.

Other pre-connected files

In order to retain compatibility with Fortran 66, many systems provide other pre-connected files. It used to be customary to have unit 5 connected to the card-reader, and unit 6 to the line printer. Other units were usually connected to disk files with appropriate names: thus unit 39 might be connected to a file called FTN039.DAT or even TAPE39. These pre-connections are completely obsolete and should be ignored: an OPEN statement can supersede a pre-connection on any numbered unit. Unfortunately, these obsolete pre-connections can have unexpected side effects. If you forget to open an output file you may find that your program will run without error but that the results will be hidden on a file with one of these special names.

10.5 Error and End-of-File Conditions

Errors in most executable statements can be prevented by taking sufficient care in writing the program, but in I/O statements errors can be caused by events beyond the control of the programmer: for example through trying to open a file which no longer exists, writing to a disk which is full, or reading a data file which has been created with the wrong format. Since I/O statements are so vulnerable, Fortran provides an error-handling mechanism for them. There are actually two different ways of handling errors which may be used independently or in combination.

Firstly, you can include in the I/O control list an item of the form:

```
IOSTAT=integer-variable
```

When the statement has executed the integer variable (or array element) it will be assigned a value representing the I/O status. If the statement has completed successfully this variable is set to zero, otherwise it is set to some other value, a positive number if an error has occurred, or a negative value if the end of an input file was detected. Since the value of this status code is system-dependent, in portable software the most you can do is to compare it to zero and, possibly, report the actual error code to the user. Thus:

```
100    WRITE(UNIT=*, FMT=*)'Enter name of input
     $    file:'
       READ(UNIT=*, FMT=*) FNAME
       OPEN(UNIT=INPUT, FILE=FNAME, STATUS='OLD',
     $    IOSTAT=KODE)
        IF(KODE .NE. 0) THEN
           WRITE(UNIT=*,FMT=*)FNAME, 'cannot be
     $    opened'
           GO TO 100
        END IF
```
This simple error-handling scheme makes the program just a little more user-friendly: if the file cannot be opened, perhaps because it does not exist, the program asks for another file-name.

The second method is to include an item of the form
```
       ERR=label
```
which causes control to be transferred to the statement attached to that label in the event of an error. This must, of course, be an executable statement and in the same program unit. For example:
```
       READ(UNIT=IN, FMT=*, ERR=999) VOLTS, AMPS
       WATTS = VOLTS * AMPS
*rest of program in here . . . . . and finally
       STOP
999    WRITE(UNIT=*,FMT=*)'Error reading VOLTS or
     $    AMPS'
       END
```
This method has its uses but is open to the same objections as the GO TO statement: it often leads to badly-structured programs with lots of arbitrary jumps.

By using both IOSTAT= and ERR= in the same statement it is possible to find out the actual error number and jump to the error-handling code. The presence of either keyword in an I/O statement will allow the program to continue after an I/O error; on most systems it also prevents an error message being issued.

The ERR= and IOSTAT= items can be used in all I/O statements. Professional programmers should make extensive use of these error-handling mechanisms to enhance the robustness and user-friendliness of their software.

There is one fairly common mistake which does not count as an error for this purpose: if you write a number to a formatted record using a field width too narrow to contain it, the field will simply be filled with asterisks.

If an error occurs in a data transfer statement then the position of the file becomes indeterminate. It may be quite difficult to locate the offending record if an error is detected when transferring a large array or using a large number of records.

End-of-file detection

A READ statement which tries to read a record beyond the end of a sequential or internal file will trigger the end-of-file condition. If an item of the form:

    IOSTAT=*integer-variable*

is included in its control-list then the status value will be returned as some *negative* number. If it includes an item of the form:

    END=*label*

then control is transferred to the labelled statement when the end-of-file condition is detected.

The END= keyword may only be used in READ statements, but it can be used in the presence of both ERR= and IOSTAT= keywords. End-of-file detection is very useful when reading a file of unknown length, but some caution is necessary. If you read several records at a time from a formatted file there is no easy way of knowing exactly where the end-of-file condition occurred. The data list items beyond that point will have their values unaltered. Note also that there is no concept of end-of-file on direct-access files: it is simply an error to read a record which does not exist, whether it is beyond the 'end' of the file or not.

Most systems provide some method for signalling end-of-file on terminal input: those based on the ASCII code often use the character which is usually produced by pressing *control/Z* on the keyboard. After an end-of-file condition has been raised in this way it may persist, preventing further terminal input to that program.

Formally, the Fortran Standard only requires Fortran systems to detect the *end-of-file* condition on external files if there is a special 'end-file' record on the end. The END FILE statement is provided specifically to write such a record. In practice, however, virtually all Fortran systems respond perfectly well when you try to read the first non-existent record, so that the END FILE statement is effectively obsolete and is not recommended for general use.

10.6 Format Specifications

Every READ or WRITE statement which uses a formatted external file or an internal file must include a format identifier. This may have any of the following forms:

FMT=★   This specifies a list-directed transfer (and is only permitted for external sequential files). Detailed rules are given in section 10.10.

FMT=*label*   The label must be attached to a FORMAT statement in the same program unit which provides the format specification.

FMT=*char-exp* The value of the character expression is a complete format specification.

FMT=*char-array* The elements of the character array contain the format specification, which may occupy as many elements of the array as are necessary.

Note that the characters 'FMT=' may be omitted if it is the second item in the I/O control list and if the unit identifier with 'UNIT=' omitted comes first.

A *format specification* consists of a pair of parentheses enclosing a list of items called *edit descriptors*. Any blanks before the left parenthesis will be ignored and (except in a FORMAT statement) all characters after the matching right parenthesis are ignored.

In most cases the format can be chosen when the program is written and the simplest option is to use a character constant:

```
      WRITE(UNIT=LP, FMT='(1X,A,F10.5)') 'Frequency =',
     $ HERTZ
```

Alternatively you can use a FORMAT statement:

```
      WRITE(UNIT=LP, FMT=915) 'Frequency=', HERTZ
 915  FORMAT(1X, A, F10.5)
```

This allows the same format to be used by more than one data-transfer statement. The FORMAT statement may also be the neater form if the specification is long and complicated, or if character-constant descriptors are involved, since the enclosing apostrophes have to be doubled up if the whole format is part of another character constant.

It is also possible to compute a format specification at run-time by using a suitable character expression. By this means you could, for example, arrange to read the format specification of a data file from the first record of the file. The program fragment below shows how to output a real number in fixed-point format (F10.2) when it is small, changing to exponential format (E18.6) when it is larger. A threshold of a million has been chosen here.

```
      CHARACTER F1*(*), F2*12, F3*(*)
*Items F1, F2, F3 hold the three parts of a format
*specification.
```

126

```
*F1 and F3 are constants, F2 is a variable.
      PARAMETER (F1 = '(1X,''Peak size ='',')
      PARAMETER (F3 = ')')
*... calculation of PEAK assumed to be in here
      IF(PEAK .LT. 1.0E6) THEN
          F2 = 'F10.2'
      ELSE
          F2 = 'E18.6'
      END IF
      WRITE(UNIT=*, FMT=F1//F2//F3) PEAK
```

Note that the apostrophes surrounding the character constant 'Peak size =' have been doubled in the PARAMETER statement because they are inside another character constant. Here are two examples of output records, the triangle represents a (normally invisible) blank:

```
△Peak△size△=△△12345.67
△Peak△size△=△△△△△0.9876543E+08
```

FORMAT statement

The FORMAT statement is classed as non-executable and can, in principle, go almost anywhere in the program unit. A FORMAT statement can, of course, be continued so its maximum length is 20 lines. The same FORMAT statement can be used by more than one data transfer statement and, unless it contains character constant descriptors, used for both input and output. Since it is very easy to make a mistake in matching the items in a data transfer list with the edit descriptors in the format specification, it makes sense to put the FORMAT statement as close as possible to the READ and WRITE statements which use it.

10.7 Format Edit Descriptors

There are two types of edit descriptor: data descriptors and control descriptors.

A *data descriptor* must be provided for each data item transferred by a READ or WRITE statement; the descriptors permitted depend on the data type of the item. The data descriptors all start with a letter indicating the data type followed by an unsigned integer denoting the field width, for example:

  I5   denotes an integer field 5 characters wide,
  F9.2   denotes a floating-point field 9 characters wide with 2 digits after the decimal point.

Full details of all the data descriptors are given in the next section.

The *control descriptors* are used for a variety of purposes, such as tabbing to specific columns, producing or skipping records, and controlling the transfer of subsequent numerical data. They are described fully in section 10.9.

Note that only literal constants are permitted within format specifications, not named constants or variables.

10.8 Format Data Descriptors

A data descriptor must be provided for each data item present (or implied) in a data transfer list. Real, double precision and complex items may use any of the E, F or G descriptors, but in all other cases the data type must match. Two floating-point descriptors are needed for each complex value.

Table 10.1 Format data descriptors

Data type	Data descriptors
Integer	Iw, I$w.m$
Real, Double Precision or Complex	E$w.d$. E$w.d$Ee. F$w.d$, G$w.d$ G$w.d$Ee
Logical	Lw
Character	A, Aw

The letters w, m, d and e used with these data descriptors represent unsigned integer constants; w and e must be greater than zero.

- w is the total field width.
- m is the minimum number of digits produced on output.
- d is the number of digits after the decimal point.
- e is the number of digits used for the exponent.

Any data descriptor can be preceded by a repeat-count (also an unsigned integer), thus:

    3F6.0   is equivalent to   F6.0,F6.0,F6.0

This facility is particularly useful when handling arrays.

General rules for numeric input/output

Numbers are always converted using the decimal number base: there is no provision in Standard Fortran for transfers in other number bases such as octal or hexadecimal. More complicated conversions such as these can be performed with the aid of internal files.

On output, numbers are generally right-justified in the specified field; leading blanks are supplied where necessary. Negative values are always preceded by a minus sign (for which space must be allowed in the field); zero is always unsigned; the SP and SS descriptors control whether positive numbers are to be preceded by a plus sign or not. A number which is too large to fit into its field will appear instead as a set of w asterisks.

On input numbers should be right-justified in each field. All forms of constant permitted in a Fortran program can safely be used in an input field of the corresponding type, as long there are no embedded or trailing blanks. Leading blanks are always ignored; a field which is entirely blank will be read as zero. The treatment of embedded and trailing blanks can be controlled with the BN and BZ descriptors. The rules here are another relic of very early Fortran systems.

When reading a file which has been connected by means of an OPEN statement (provided it does not contain BLANK='ZERO') all embedded and trailing blanks in numeric input fields are treated as *nulls*, i.e. they are ignored. In all other cases, such as input from the *standard pre-connected file* or from an internal file, embedded and trailing blanks are treated as *zeros*. These defaults can be altered with the BN and BZ control descriptors.

It is hard to imagine any circumstances in which it is desirable to interpret embedded blanks as zeros; the default settings are particularly ill-chosen since numbers entered by a user at a terminal are often left-justified and may appear to be padded out with zeros. Errors from this source can be avoided by using BN at the beginning of all input format specifications.

Integer data (Iw, Iw.m)

An integer value written with I*w* appears right-justified in a field of *w* characters with leading blanks. I*w.m* is similar but ensures that at least *m* digits will appear even if leading zeros are necessary. This is useful, for instance, to output the times in hours and minutes:

```
      NHOURS = 8
      MINUTE = 6
      WRITE(UNIT=*, FMT='(I4.2, I2.2)') NHOURS,
     $  MINUTE
```

The output record (with △ used to denote a blank) is:

On input I*w* and I*w.m* are identical. Note that an integer field must not contain a decimal point, exponent or any punctuation characters such as commas.

Floating point data (E*w.d*, E*w.d*E*e*, F*w.d*, G*w.d*, G*w.d*E*e*)

Data of any of the floating-point types (Real, Double Precision and Complex) may be transferred using any of the descriptors E, F or G. For each *complex* number *two* descriptors must be provided, one for each component; these components may be separated, if required, by control descriptors. On output numbers are rounded to the specified number of digits. All floating-point data transfers are affected by the setting of the *scale-factor*; this is initially zero but can be altered by the P control descriptor, as explained in section 10.9.

Output using F*w.d* produces a fixed-point value in a field of *w* characters with exactly *d* digits after the decimal point. The decimal point is present even if *w* is zero, so that if a sign is produced there is only space for, at most, *w*−2 digits before the decimal point. If it is really important to suppress the decimal point in numbers with no fractional part one way is to use a format specification of the form (F15.0,TL1...) so that the next field starts one place to the left and overwrites the decimal point. Another way is to copy the number to an integer variable and write it with an I descriptor, but note the limited range of integers on most systems. F format is especially convenient in tabular layouts since the decimal points will line up in successive records, but it is not suitable for very large or small numbers.

Output with E*w.d* produces a number in exponential or 'scientific' notation. The mantissa will be between 0.1 and 1 (if the *scale-factor* is zero). The form E*w.d*E*e* specifies that there should be exactly e digits in the exponent. This form *must* be used if the exponent will have more than three digits (although this problem does not arise on machines on which the number range is too small). E format can be used to handle numbers of any magnitude. The disadvantage is that exceptionally large or small values do not stand out very well in the resulting columns of figures.

G*w.d* is the general-purpose descriptor: if the value is greater than 0.1 but not too large to fit it the field it will be written using a fixed-point format with *d* digits in total and with 4 blanks at the end of the field; otherwise it is equivalent to E*w.d* format. The form G*w.d*E*e* allows you to specify the length of the exponent; if a fixed-point format is chosen there are *e*+2 blanks at the end.

The next example shows the different properties of these three formats on output:

```
X = 123.456789
Y = 0.09876543
WRITE(UNIT=*, FMT='(E12.5, F12.5, G12.5)')
$    X,X,X,  Y,Y,Y
```

produces two records (with △ representing the blank):

```
△0.12346E+03△△△123.45679△△123.46△△△△
△0.98766E-01△△△△△0.09877△0.98766E-01
```

On input all the E, F and G descriptors have identical effects: if the input field contains an explicit decimal point it always takes precedence, otherwise the last *d* digits are taken as the decimal fraction. If an exponent is used it may be preceded by E or D (but the exponent letter is optional if the exponent is signed). If the input field provides more digits than the internal storage can utilise, the extra precision is ignored. It is usually best to use (F*w*.0) which will cope with all common floating-point or even integer forms.

Logical data (L*w*)

When a logical value is written with L*w* the field will contain the letter T or F preceded by (*w*−1) blanks. On input the field must contain the letter T or F; the letter may be preceded by a decimal point and any number of blanks. Characters after the T or F are ignored. Thus the forms .TRUE. and .FALSE. are acceptable.

Character data (A and A*w*)

If the A descriptor is used without an explicit field-width then the length of the character item in the data-transfer list determines it. This is generally what is required but note that the position of the remaining items in the record will change if the length of the character item is altered.

If it is important to use fixed column layouts the form A*w* may be preferred: it always uses a field *w* characters wide. On output if the actual length *len* is less than *w* the value is right-justified in the field and preceded by (*w* − *len*) blanks; otherwise only the first *w* characters are output, the rest are ignored. On input if the length *len* is less than *w* then the right-most *len* characters are used, otherwise *w* characters will be read into the character variable with (*len*−*w*) blanks appended.

10.9 Format Control Descriptors

Control descriptors do not correspond to any item in the data-transfer list: they are obeyed when the format scan reaches that point in the list. A format specification consisting of nothing but control descriptors is valid only if the READ or WRITE statement has an empty data-transfer list.

Table 10.2 Format control descriptors

Control function	Control descriptions
Skip to next record	/
Move to specified column position	Tn, TLn, TRn, nX
Output a character constant	'any char string'
Stop format scan if data list empty	:
Produce/suppress + before positive numbers	SP, SS, S
Treat blanks as nulls/zeros	BN, BZ
Set scale factor for numeric transfers	kP

Here n and k are integer constants, k may have a sign but n must be non-zero and unsigned. The control descriptors such as SP, BN, kP affect all numbers transferred subsequently. The settings are unaffected by *forced reversion* but the system defaults are restored at the start of the next READ or WRITE operation.

Any list of edit descriptors may be enclosed in parentheses and preceded by an integer constant as a repetition count, e.g.

    2(I2.2, '-'),I2.2

is equivalent to

    I2.2, '-', I2.2, '-', I2.2

These sub-lists can be nested to any reasonable depth, but the presence of internal pairs of parentheses can have special effects when *forced reversion* takes place, as explained later.

Commas may be omitted between items in the following special cases: either side of a slash (/) or colon (:) descriptor, and after a scale-factor (kP) if it immediately precedes a D, E, F or G descriptor.

Record control (/)

The slash descriptor (/) starts a new record on output or skips to a new record on input, ignoring anything left on the current record. On a text file a record normally corresponds to a line of text. Note that a formatted transfer always processes at least one record: if the format contains N slashes then a total of (N+1) records are processed. With N consecutive slashes in an output format there will be (N−1) blank lines; on input then (N−1) lines will be ignored. Note that if a formatted sequential file is sent to a printer the first character of every record may be used for carriage-control (see section 10.11). It is good practice to put 1X at the beginning of every format specification and after every slash to ensure single line spacing. Here, for example, there is a blank line after the column headings.

```
       WRITE(UNIT=LP, FMT=95) (NYEAR(I), POP(I),
    $   I=1,NYEARS)
95     FORMAT(1X,'Year Population', //, 100(1X, I4,
    $   F12.0,/))
```

Column position control (T*n*, TL*n*, TR*n*, *n*X)

These descriptors cause subsequent values to be transferred starting at a different column position in the record. They can, for instance, be used to set up a table with headings positioned over each column. In all these descriptors the value of *n* must be 1 or more. Columns are numbered from 1 on the left (but remember that column 1 may be used for carriage-control if the output is sent to a printer).

- T*n*   causes subsequent output to start at column *n*.
- TR*n* causes a shift to the right by *n* columns.
- TL*n* causes a shift to the left by *n* columns (but it will not move the position to the left of column 1).
- *n*X   is exactly equivalent to TR*n*.

On input TL*n* can be used to re-read the same field again, possibly using a different data descriptor. On output these descriptors do not necessarily have any direct effect on the record: they do not cause any existing characters to be replaced by blanks, but when the record is complete any column positions embedded in the record which are still unset will be replaced by blanks. Thus:

```
       WRITE(UNIT=LP, FMT=9000)
9000   FORMAT('A', TR1000, TL950, 'Z')
```

will cause a record of 52 characters to be output, the middle 50 of them blanks.

Character constant output ('string')

The character constant descriptor can only be used with WRITE statements: the character string is simply copied to the output record. As in all character constants an apostrophe can be represented in the string by two successive apostrophes, and blanks are significant.

Sign control (SP, SS, S)

After SP has been used, positive numbers will be written with a leading + sign; after SS has been used the + sign is suppressed. The S descriptor restores the initial default which is system-dependent. These descriptors have no effect on numerical input. The initial default is restored at the start of every new formatted transfer.

Blank control (BN, BZ)

After BN is used all embedded and trailing blanks in numerical input fields are treated as nulls, i.e. ignored. After BZ they are treated as zeros. These descriptors have no effect on numerical output. The initial default, which depends on the BLANK= item in the OPEN statement, is restored at the start of every new formatted transfer.

Scale factor control (kP)

The scale factor can be used to introduce a scaling by any power of 10 between internal and external values when E, F or G descriptors are used. In principle this could be useful when dealing with data which are too large or too small for the exponent range of the floating-point data types of the machine, but other difficulties usually make this impracticable. The scale factor can result in particularly insidious errors when used with F descriptors and should be avoided by all sensible programmers. The rules are as follows.

The initial scale factor in each formatted transfer is zero. If the descriptor kP is used, where k is a small (optionally signed) integer, then it is set to k. It affects all subsequent floating point values transferred by the statement. On input there is no effect if the input field contains an explicit exponent, otherwise

$$\text{internal-value} = \text{external-value} / 10^k$$

On output the effect depends on the descriptor used. With E descriptors the decimal point is moved k places to the right and the exponent reduced by k so the effective value is unaltered. With F descriptors there is always a scaling:

$$\textit{external-value} = \textit{internal-value} \star 10^k$$

With G descriptors the scale-factor is ignored if the value is in the range for F-type output, otherwise it has the same effects as with E descriptors.

Scan control (:) and forced reversion

The list of edit descriptors is scanned from left to right (apart from the effect of parentheses) starting at the beginning of the list whenever a new data transfer statement is executed. The action of the I/O system depends jointly on the next edit descriptor and the next item in data-transfer list. If a *data descriptor* comes next then the next data item is transferred if one exists, otherwise the format scan comes to an end. If a colon descriptor (:) comes next and the data-transfer list is empty the format scan ends, otherwise the descriptor has no effect. If any other *control descriptor* comes next then it is obeyed whether or not the data-transfer list is empty.

If the format list is exhausted when there are still more items in the data-transfer list then *forced reversion* occurs: the file is positioned at the beginning of the next record and the format list is scanned again, starting at the left-parenthesis matching the last preceding right-parenthesis. If this is preceded by a repeat-count then this count is re-used. If there is no preceding right-parenthesis then the whole format is re-used. Forced reversion has no effect upon the settings for scale-factor, sign or blank control. Forced reversion can be useful when reading or writing an array contained on a sequence of records since it is not necessary to know how many records there are in total, but when producing printed output it is easy to forget that a carriage-control character is required for each record, even those produced by forced reversion.

10.10 List-Directed Formatting

List-directed output

List-directed output uses a format chosen by the system according to the data type of the item. The exact layout is system-dependent, but the general rules are as follows.

Each WRITE statement starts a new record; additional records are produced when necessary. Each record starts with a single blank to provide carriage-control on printing. Arithmetic data types are converted to decimal values with the number of digits appropriate for the internal precision. *Integer* values will not have a decimal point; the system may choose fixed-point or exponential (scientific) form for *floating-point* values depending on their magnitude. *Complex* values are enclosed in parentheses with a comma separating the two parts.

Logical values are output as a single letter, either T or F.

Character values are output without enclosing apostrophes; if a character string is too long for one record it may be continued on the next.

Except for character values, each item is followed by at least one blank or a comma (or both) to separate it from the next value.

List-directed input

The rules for list-directed input effectively allow free-format entry for numerical data. Each READ statement starts with a new record and reads as many records as are necessary to satisfy its data-transfer list. The input records must contain a suitable sequence of *values* and *separators*.

The values may be given in any form which would be acceptable in a Fortran program for a constant of the corresponding type, except that embedded blanks are only permitted in character values. When reading a *real* or *double-precision* value an *integer* constant will be accepted; when reading a *logical* value only the letter T or F is required (a preceding dot and any following characters will be ignored). Note that a character constant must be enclosed in apostrophes and a complex constant must be enclosed in parentheses with a comma between the two components. If a character constant is too long to fit on one record it may be continued on to the next; the two parts of a complex constant may also be given on two records.

The separator between successive values must be one or more blanks, or a comma, or both. A new record may start at any point at which a blank would be permitted.

If several successive items are to have the same value a repetition factor can be used: this has the form *n★constant* where *n* is an unsigned integer. Blanks are not allowed either side of the asterisk.

Two successive commas represent a null value: the corresponding variable in the READ statement has its value unchanged. It is also possible to use the form $n\star$ to represent a set of n null values.

A slash (/) may be used instead of an item separator; it has the effect of completing the current READ without further input; all remaining items in its data transfer list are unchanged in value.

List-directed output files are generally compatible with list-directed input, unless they contain *character* items, which will not have the enclosing apostrophes which are required on input.

10.11 Carriage-Control and Printing

Although a format specification allows complete control over the layout of each line of text, it does not include any way of controlling *pagination*. The only way to do this is by using a unique and extraordinary mechanism dating back to the earliest days of Fortran. Even if you are not concerned with pagination you still need to know about the carriage-control convention since it is liable to affect every text file you produce.

Whenever formatted output is sent to a 'printer', the first character of every record is removed and used to control the vertical spacing. This *carriage-control* character must be one of the four listed in the Table 10.3.

Table 10.3 Carriage control characters

Character	Vertical spacing before printing
blank	Advance one line
0	Advance two lines
1	Advance to top of next page
+	No advance

An empty record is treated as if it started with a single blank. For example, these statements start a new page with a page number at the top and a title on the third line:

```
      WRITE(LP, 55) NUMBER, 'Report and Accounts'
55    FORMAT('1PAGE', I4, /, '0', A)
```

This carriage-control convention is an absurd relic which causes a multitude of problems in practice. Firstly, systems differ in what they call a 'printer': it may or may not apply to visual display terminals or to text initially saved on a disk file and later printed out. Some operating systems have a special file type for Fortran formatted output which is treated differently by printers (and terminals). Others have been known to chop off the first character of *all* files sent to the system printer so that special utilities are needed to print ordinary text.

To be on the safe side you should always provide an explicit carriage-control character at the start of each format specification and after each slash. Special care is needed in formats which use *forced reversion*. Normal single spacing is obtained with a blank, conveniently produced by the '1X' edit descriptor. If you forget and accidentally print a number at the start of each record with a leading digit 1 then each record will start a new page.

The effect of '+' as a carriage-control character would be more useful if its effects were more predictable. Some devices over-print the previous record (allowing the formation of composite characters like $\neq$), others append to it, and some (including many visual display terminals) erase what was there before. In portable software there is no alternative but to ignore the '+' case altogether.

Standard Fortran can only use the four carriage-control characters listed in Table 10.3 but many systems use other symbols for special formatting purposes, such as setting vertical spacing, changing fonts, and so on. One extension which is widely available is the use of the currency symbol '$' to suppress carriage-return at the end of the line. This can be useful when producing terminal prompts as it allows the reply to be entered on the same line. There is, unfortunately, no way of doing this in Standard Fortran.

The rules for *list-directed* output ensure that the lines are single-spaced by requiring at least one blank at the start of every record.

10.12 Input/Output Statements and Keywords

The I/O statements fall into three groups:
- The data transfer statements READ and WRITE.
- The file connection statements OPEN, CLOSE and INQUIRE.
- The file positioning statements REWIND and BACKSPACE.

All these statements have a similar general form (except that only the READ and WRITE statements can have a data-transfer list):

```
operation ( control-list ) data-list
```

The items in each list are separated by commas. Those in the control-list are usually specified by keywords, in which case the order does not matter, although it is conventional to have the unit identifier first. For compatibility with Fortran 66, if the unit identifier does come first then the keyword UNIT= may be omitted. Furthermore, when this keyword is omitted in READ and WRITE statements and the format identifier is second its keyword may also be omitted. Thus these two statements are exactly equivalent:

```
READ(UNIT=1, FMT=*, ERR=999) AMPS, VOLTS, HERTZ
READ(1, *, ERR=999) AMPS, VOLTS, HERTZ
```

Use of this abbreviated form is a matter of taste: for the sake of clarity the keywords will all be shown in other examples.

Many of the keywords in the control-list can take a character expression as an argument: in such cases any trailing blanks in the value will be ignored. This makes it easy to use character variables to specify file names and characteristics without the need for exact length agreement.

There is one general restriction on expressions used in all I/O statements: they must not call external functions which themselves execute further I/O statements. This restriction avoids the possibility of recursive calls to the I/O system.

10.13 OPEN Statement

The OPEN statement is used to connect a file to an I/O unit and describe its characteristics. It can open an existing file or create a new one. If the unit is already connected to another file then this is closed before the new connection is made, so that it is impossible to connect two files simultaneously to the same unit. It is an error to try to connect more than one unit simultaneously to the same file. In the special case in which the unit and file are already connected to each other, the OPEN statement may be used to alter the properties of the connection, although in practice only the BLANK= (and sometimes RECL=) values can be changed in this way.

The Fortran Standard does not specify the file position when an existing sequential file is opened. Although most operating systems behave sensibly, in portable software a REWIND statement should be used to ensure that the file is rewound before you read it.

The general form of the OPEN statement is just:

```
OPEN( control-list )
```

The control-list can contain any of the following items in any order:

UNIT=*integer-expression*

The integer expression species the I/O unit number which must be zero or above; the upper limit is system-dependent, typically 99 or 255. The unit identifier must always be given, there is no default value.

STATUS=*character-expression*

The character expression describes or specifies the file status. The value must be one of:
- 'OLD'   The file must exist.
- 'NEW'   The file must not already exist, a new file is created.
- 'SCRATCH' An unnamed temporary file is created; it is deleted automatically when the program exits.
- 'UNKNOWN' The effect is system-dependent, but usually means that an old file will be used if one exists, otherwise a new file will be created.

The default value is 'UNKNOWN', but it is unwise to omit the STATUS keyword because the effect of 'UNKNOWN' is so ill-defined.

FILE=*character-expression*

The character expression specifies the file-name (but any trailing blanks will be ignored). The forms of file-name acceptable are system-dependent: a complete file-specification on some operating systems may include the device, user-name, directory path, file-type, version number, etc., and may require various punctuation marks to separate these. In portable software, where the name has to be acceptable to a variety of operating systems, short and simple names should be used. Alternatively the FILE= identifier may be a character variable (or array element) so that the user can choose a file-name at run-time. There is no default for the file-name so one should be specified in all cases unless STATUS='SCRATCH' in which case the file must not be named.

ACCESS=*character-expression*

The character expression specifies the file access method. The value may be either:
- 'SEQUENTIAL' a sequential file: this is the default.

- 'DIRECT'   a direct-access file: in this case the RECL= keyword is also needed.

FORM=*character-expression*

The character expression specifies the record format. The value may be either:

   'FORMATTED'   the default for a sequential file.
   'UNFORMATTED'   the default for a direct-access file.

RECL=*integer-expression*

The integer expression specifies the record length. This must be given for a direct-access file but not otherwise. The record-length is measured in characters for a formatted file, but is in system-dependent units (often numeric storage units) for an unformatted file.

BLANK=*character-expression*

The character expression specifies how embedded and trailing blanks in numerical input fields of formatted files are to be treated (in the absence of explicit format descriptors BN or BZ). The value may be either:

   'NULL' blanks treated as nulls, i.e. ignored: the default.
   'ZERO' blanks treated as zeros.

The default value is likely to be the sensible choice in all cases.

IOSTAT=*integer-variable*

The integer variable (or array element) returns the I/O status code after execution of the OPEN statement. This will be zero value if no error has occurred, otherwise it will return a system-dependent positive value.

ERR=*label*

The label must be that of an executable statement in the same program unit to which control will be transferred in the event of an error.

10.14 CLOSE Statement

The CLOSE statement is used to close a file and break its connection to a unit. The unit and the file (if it still exists) are then free for re-use in any way. If the specified unit is not connected to a file the statement has no effect. The general form of the statement is:

CLOSE(*control-list*)

where the control list may contain the following items:

UNIT=*integer-expression*

The unit number must be specified as in the OPEN statement.

DISP=*character-expression*

The expression must have a value of either:
   'KEEP'   the file is preserved, or
   'DELETE' the file is deleted after closure.
The default is DISP='KEEP' except for files opened with STATUS= 'SCRATCH': such files are always deleted after closure and DISP= 'KEEP' is not permitted.

IOSTAT=*integer-variable*
ERR=*label*

These are both permitted, as in the OPEN statement (but not much can go wrong with a CLOSE statement).

10.15 INQUIRE Statement

The INQUIRE statement can be used in two slightly different forms:

      INQUIRE(UNIT=*integer-expression*, *inquire-list*)
or   INQUIRE(FILE=*character-expression*, *inquire-list*)

The first form, an *inquire by unit*, returns information about the unit and, if it is connected to a file, about the file as well. If it is not connected to a file then most of the arguments will be undefined or return a value of 'UNKNOWN' as appropriate.

The second form, *inquire by file*, can always be used to find out whether a named file exists, i.e. can be opened by a Fortran program. Any trailing blanks in the character expression are ignored, and the forms of file-name acceptable are, as in the OPEN statement, system-dependent. If the file exists and is connected to a unit then much more information can be obtained.

The inquire-list may contain any of the items below. Note that all of them (except for ERR=*label*) return information by assigning a value to a named variable (or array element). The normal rules of assignment statements apply, so that character items may have any reasonable length and will return a value which is padded out with blanks to its declared length if necessary.

```
IOSTAT=integer-variable
ERR=label
```

These can be used in the same way as in OPEN or CLOSE; note that they detect errors during the execution of the INQUIRE statement itself, and do not reflect the state of the file or unit which is the subject of the inquiry.

```
EXIST=logical-variable
```

The variable is set to .TRUE. if the specified unit or file *exists*, or .FALSE. if it does not. A unit exists if it has a number in the permitted range. A file exists if it can be used in an OPEN statement. A file may appear not to exist merely because the operating system prevents its use, for example because a password is needed or because some other user has already opened it.

```
OPENED=logical-variable
```

The variable is set to .TRUE. if the specified unit (or file) is currently connected to a file (or unit) in the program.

```
NUMBER=integer-variable
```

The variable returns the unit number of a file which is connected; otherwise it becomes undefined.

NAME=*character-variable*

The variable returns the file-name if the file has a name; if not it becomes undefined. In the case of an inquire by file the name may not be the same as that specified using FILE= (because a device-name or directory path may have been added) but the name returned will always be suitable for use in an OPEN statement.

ACCESS=*character-variable*

The variable returns the record access-method, either 'SEQUENTIAL' or 'DIRECT' if the file is connected; if it is not connected the variable becomes undefined.

SEQUENTIAL=*character-variable*

The variable returns 'YES' if the file can be opened for sequential access, 'NO' if it cannot, and 'UNKNOWN' otherwise.

DIRECT=*character-variable*

The variable returns 'YES' if the file can be opened for direct access, 'NO' if it cannot, and 'UNKNOWN' otherwise.

FORM=*character-variable*

The variable returns 'FORMATTED' if the file is connected for formatted access, 'UNFORMATTED' if it is connected for unformatted access, or becomes undefined if there is no connection.

FORMATTED=*character-variable*

The variable returns 'YES' if formatted access is permitted, 'NO' if it is not, or 'UNKNOWN' otherwise.

UNFORMATTED=*character-variable*

The variable returns 'YES' if unformatted access is permitted, 'NO' if it is not, or 'UNKNOWN' otherwise.

RECL=*integer-variable*

The variable returns the record length if the file is connected for direct-access but becomes undefined otherwise. Note that the units are characters for formatted files, but are system- dependent for unformatted files.

NEXTREC=*integer-variable*

The variable returns a number which is one higher than the last record read or written if the file is connected for direct access. If it is connected for direct access but no records have been transferred, the variable returns one. If the file is not connected for direct access the variable becomes undefined.

BLANK=*character-variable*

The variable returns 'NULL' or 'BLANK' if the file is connected for formatted access according to the way embedded and trailing blanks are to be treated. In other cases it becomes undefined.

10.16 READ and WRITE Statements

The READ statement reads information from one or more records on a file into a list of variables, array elements, etc. The WRITE statement writes information from a list of items which may include variables, arrays and expressions, and produces one or more records on a file. Each READ or WRITE statement can only transfer one record on an unformatted file but on formatted files, including internal files, more than one record may be transferred, depending on the contents of the format specification.

The two statements have the same general form:

```
READ( control-list ) data-list
WRITE( control-list ) data-list
```

The *control list* must contain a unit identifier; the other items may be optional depending on the type of file. The *data list* is also optional: if it is absent the statement transfers one record (or possibly more under the control of a format specification).

Unit identifier

This may have any of the following forms:

UNIT=*integer-expression* The value of the expression must be zero or greater and must refer to a valid I/O unit.

UNIT=★ For the standard pre-connected input or output file.

UNIT=*internal-file* The *internal-file* may be a variable, array-element, substring, or array of type character (see section 10.3)

Note that the keyword UNIT= is optional if the unit identifier is the first item in the control list.

Format identifier

A format identifier must be provided when using a formatted (or internal) file but not otherwise. It may have any of the following forms:

FMT=*label* The label of a FORMAT statement in the same program unit.

FMT=*format* The *format* may be a character expression or character array containing a complete format specification (section 10.6).

FMT=★ For list-directed formatting (section 10.10).

Note that the keyword FMT= is also optional if the format identifier is the second item in the control list and the first item is a unit identifier specified without its keyword.

Record number

A record number identifier must be provided for direct-access files but not otherwise. It has the form:

REC=*integer-expression*

The record number must be greater than zero; for READ it must refer to a record which exists.

Error and end-of-file identifiers

These may be provided in any combination, but END=*label* is only valid when reading a sequential or internal file. See section 10.5 for more information.

```
END=label
ERR=label
IOSTAT=integer-variable
```

Data list

The *data list* of a READ statement may contain variables, array-elements, character-substrings, or complete arrays of any data type. An array-name without subscripts represents all the elements of the array; this is not permitted for assumed-size dummy arguments in procedures (because the array size is indeterminate). The list may also contain *implied DO-loops* (explained below).

The *data list* of a WRITE statement may contain any of the items permitted in a READ statement and in addition expressions of any data type. As in all I/O statements, expressions must not themselves involve the execution of other I/O statements.

Implied DO-loops

The simplest and most efficient way to read or write all the elements of an array is to put its name, unsubscripted, in the data-transfer list. In the case of a multi-dimensional array the elements will be transferred in the normal storage sequence, with the first subscript varying most rapidly.

An implied-DO loop allows the elements to be transferred selectively or in some non-standard order. The rules for an implied-DO are similar to that of an ordinary DO-loop but the loop forms a single item in the data-transfer list and is enclosed by a pair of parentheses rather than by DO and CONTINUE statements. For example:

```
      READ(UNIT=*, FMT=*)  (ARRAY(I), I= IMIN, IMAX)
      WRITE(UNIT=*,FMT=15) (M, X(M), Y(M), M= 1,101,5)
15    FORMAT(1X, I6, 2F12.3)
```

A multi-dimensional array can be printed out in a transposed form. The next example outputs an array X(100,5) but with 5 elements across and 100 lines vertically:

```
      WRITE(UNIT=*, FMT=5) (I,I=1,5),
     $  (L,(X(L,I),I=1,5),L=1,100)
5     FORMAT(1X,'LINE', 5I10, 100(/,1X,I4, 5F10.2))
```

The first loop writes headings for the five columns, then the double loop writes a line-number for each line followed by five array elements. Note that the parentheses have to be matched and that a comma is needed after the inner right-parenthesis since the inner loop is just an item in the list contained in the outer loop.

The implied DO-loop has the general form:

(*data-list, loop-variable = start, limit, step*)

where the rules for the *start*, *limit* and *step* values are exactly as in an ordinary DO statement. The loop variable (normally an integer) may be used within the data-list and this list may, in turn, include further complete implied-DO lists.

If an error or end-of-file condition occurs in an implied DO-loop then the loop-control variable will be undefined on exit; this means that an explicit DO-loop is required to read an indefinite list of data records and exit with knowledge of how many items were actually input.

10.17 REWIND and BACKSPACE Statements

These file-positioning statements may only be used on external sequential files; most systems will restrict them to files stored on suitable peripheral devices such as disks or tapes.

REWIND repositions a file to the beginning of information so that the next READ statement will read the first record; if a WRITE statement is used after REWIND all existing records on the file are destroyed. REWIND has no effect if the file is already rewound. If a REWIND statement is used on a unit which is connected but does not exist (e.g. a pre-connected output file) it creates the file.

BACKSPACE moves the file position back by one record so that the record can be re-read or over-written. There is no effect if the file is already positioned at the beginning of information but it is an error to back-space a file which does not exist. It is also illegal to back-space over records written by list-directed formatting (because the number of records produced each time is system-dependent). A few operating systems find it difficult to implement the BACKSPACE statement directly and actually manage it only by rewinding the file and spacing forward to the appropriate record. It is sometimes possible to avoid backspacing a file by allocating buffers within the program and, for a formatted file, using internal file READ and WRITE statements.

These statements have a similar general form:

```
REWIND( control-list )
BACKSPACE( control-list )
```

where the control list may contain:

```
UNIT=integer-expression
IOSTAT=integer-variable
ERR=label
```

The unit identifier is compulsory, the others optional. If only the unit identifier is used then (for compatibility with Fortran 66) an abbreviated form of the statement is permitted:

```
REWIND integer-expression
BACKSPACE integer-expression
```

where the integer expression identifies the unit number.

11 The DATA Statement

The DATA statement is used to specify initial values for variables and array elements. The DATA statement is non-executable, but in a *main program* unit it has the same effect as a set of assignment statements at the very beginning of the program. Thus in a main program a DATA statement like this:

```
DATA LINES/625/, FREQ/50.0/, NAME/'PAL'/
```

could replace several assignment statements:

```
LINES = 625
FREQ  = 50.0
NAME  = 'PAL'
```

This is more convenient, especially when initialising arrays, and efficient, since the work is done when the program is loaded.

In a *procedure,* however, these two methods are not equivalent, especially in the case of items which are modified as the procedure executes. A DATA statement only sets the values once at the start of execution, whereas assignment statements will do so every time the procedure is called.

It is important to distinguish between the DATA and PARAMETER statements. The DATA statement merely specifies an initial value for a variable (or array) which may be altered during the course of execution. The PARAMETER statement specifies values for constants which cannot be changed without recompiling the program. If, however, you need an *array* of constants, for which there is no direct support in Fortran, you should use an ordinary array with a DATA statement to initialise its elements (and you must take care not to corrupt the contents afterwards).

11.1 Defined and Undefined Values

The value of each variable and array element is *undefined* at the start of execution unless it has been initialised with a DATA statement. An undefined value may only be used in executable statements in ways which cause it to become defined. An item can become defined by its use in any of the following ways:

- on the left-hand side of an assignment statement.
- as the control variable of a DO statement.
- in the input list of a READ statement.
- as the internal file identifier of a WRITE statement.
- as the I/O status identifier in an I/O statement.
- in an INQUIRE statement except as file or unit number.
- in a procedure call provided that the corresponding dummy argument is defined before the procedure returns control.

An undefined variable must not be used in any other way. Errors caused by the inadvertent use of undefined values are easy to make and sometimes have very obscure effects. It is important, therefore, to identify every item which needs to be initialised and provide a suitable set of DATA statements.

Modern operating systems often clear the area of memory into which they load a program to prevent unauthorised access to the data used in the preceding job. A few operating systems preset their memory to a bit-pattern which corresponds to an illegal numerical value: this is a very helpful diagnostic facility since whenever an undefined variable is used in an expression it generates an error at run time. Other systems merely set their memory to zero: this makes it more difficult to track down the use of undefined variables and they may only come to light when a program is transported to another system. To rely on undefined variables and arrays having an initial value of zero is to leave the program completely at the mercy of changes to the operating system.

11.2 Initialising Variables

The simplest form of the DATA statement consists of a list of the variable names each followed by a constant enclosed in a pair of slashes:

```
      DOUBLE PRECISION EPOCH
      LOGICAL OPENED
      CHARACTER INFILE*20
      DATA EPOCH/1950.0D0/, OPENED/.TRUE./,
     $     INFILE/'B:OBS.DAT'/
```

Note that DATA statements must follow all specification statements. An alternative form is to give a complete list of names first and follow it by a separate list of constants:

```
      DATA EPOCH, OPENED, INFILE / 1950.0D0, .TRUE.,
     'B:OBS.DAT'/
```

When there are many items to be initialised it is a matter of taste whether to use several DATA statements or to use one with many continuation lines. It is, of course, illegal to have the same item initialised twice.

Character variables can be initialised in sections using the substring notation if this is more convenient:

```
      CHARACTER*52 LETTER
      DATA LETTER(1:26)/'ABCDEFGHIJKLMNOPQRSTUVWXYZ'/,
     $     LETTER(27:) /'abcdefghijklmnopqrstuvwxyz'/
```

If the length of the character constant differs from that of the variable then the string is truncated or padded with blanks as in an assignment statement. The type conversion rules of assignment statements also apply to arithmetic items in DATA statements.

11.3 Initialising Arrays

There are several ways of using DATA statements to initialise arrays, all of them simpler and more efficient than the equivalent set of DO-loops. Perhaps the most common requirement is to initialise all the elements of an array: in this case the array name can appear without subscripts. If several of the elements are to have the same initial value a *repeat count* can precede any constant:

```
      REAL FLUX(1000)
      DATA FLUX / 512*0.0, 488*-1.0 /
```

The total number of constants must equal the number of array elements. The constants correspond to the elements in the array in the normal storage sequence; that is, with the first subscript varying most rapidly.

Named constants are permitted, but not constant expressions. The repeat count may be a literal or named integer constant. To initialise a multi-dimensional array with parameterised array bounds it is necessary to define another integer constant to hold the total number of elements:

```
      PARAMETER (NX = 800, NY = 360, NTOTAL = NX * NY)
      DOUBLE PRECISION SCREEN(NX,NY), ZERO
      PARAMETER (ZERO = 0.0D0)
      DATA SCREEN / NTOTAL * ZERO /
```

If only a few array elements are to be initialised they can be listed individually:

```
REAL SPARSE(50,50)
DATA SPARSE(1,1), SPARSE(50,50) / 1.0, 99.99999/
```

The third, and most complicated, option is to use an *implied-DO loop*. This operates in much the same way as an implied-DO in an I/O statement:

```
INTEGER ODD(10)
DATA (ODD(I),I=1,10,2)/ 5 * 43/
DATA (ODD(I),I=2,10,2)/ 5 * 0 /
```

This example has initialised all the odd numbered elements to 43 and all the even numbered elements to zero. Note that the loop control variable (I in this example) has a scope which does not extend outside the section of the DATA statement in which it is used. Any integer variable may be used as a loop control index in a DATA statement without effects elsewhere; the value of I itself is not defined by these statements.

When initialising part of a multi-dimensional array it may occasionally be useful to nest DO-loops like this:

```
DOUBLE PRECISION FIELD(5,5)
DATA ((FIELD(I,J),I=1,J), J=1,5) / 15 * -1.0D0/
```

This specifies initial values only for the upper triangle of the square array FIELD.

11.4 DATA Statements in Procedures

In procedures, DATA statements perform a role for which assignment statements are no substitute. It is quite often necessary to arrange for some action to be carried out at the start of the first call but not subsequently, such as opening a file, or initialising a variable or array which accumulates information during subsequent calls.

If information is preserved in a local variable or array from one invocation to another, a SAVE statement (described in section 9.11) is also needed. Indeed, in general any object initialised in a DATA statement in a procedure also needs to be named in a SAVE statement unless its value is never altered.

In the next example the procedure opens a data file on its first call, using a logical variable OPENED to remember the state of the file.

```
      SUBROUTINE LOOKUP(INDEX, RECORD)
      INTEGER INDEX
      REAL RECORD
      LOGICAL OPENED
      SAVE OPENED
      DATA OPENED / .FALSE. /
*On first call OPENED is false so open the file.
      IF(.NOT. OPENED) THEN
          OPEN(UNIT=57, FILE='HIDDEN.DAT',
     $        STATUS='OLD', ACCESS='DIRECT', RECL=100)
          OPENED = .TRUE.
      END IF
      READ(UNIT=57, REC=INDEX) RECORD
      END
```

Here, for simplicity, the I/O unit number is a literal constant. The procedure would be more modular if the unit number were also an argument of the procedure or if it contained some code, using the INQUIRE statement, to determine for itself a suitable unused unit number.

There is, of course, no corresponding way to determine which is the *last* call to the procedure so that the file can be closed, but this is not strictly necessary as the Fortran system closes all files automatically when the program exits.

Note that DATA statements cannot be used to initialise variables or arrays which are dummy arguments of a procedure, nor the variable in a function which has the same name as the function.

11.5 General Rules

The general form of the DATA statement is:

```
      DATA nlist / clist /, nlist / clist /, ...
```

Where: *nlist* is a list of variable names, array names, substring names, and *implied-DO* lists.

clist is a list of items which may be literal or named constants or either of these preceded by a repeat-count and an asterisk. The repeat-count can also be an unsigned integer constant or named constant.

The comma which precedes each list of names except the first is optional. An *implied-DO* list has the general form:

```
(dlist, intvar = start, limit, step)
```

Where: *dlist* is a list of implied-DO lists and array elements.
intvar is an integer variable called the loop-control variable.
start, *limit* and *step* are integer expressions in which all the operands must be integer constants or loop-control variables of outer implied-DO lists.

DATA statements cannot be used to initialise items in the blank common block; items in named common blocks can only be initialised within a BLOCK DATA program unit (see section 12.4).

The DATA statements in each program unit must follow all specification statements but they can be interspersed with executable statements and statement function statements. It is, however, best to follow the usual practice of putting all DATA statements before any of the executable statements.

12   Common Blocks

A common block is a list of variables and arrays stored in a named area which may be accessed directly in more than one program unit. Common blocks are mainly used to transfer information from one program unit to another; they can be used as an alternative to argument-list transfers or in addition to them.

Common blocks are sometimes used to fit large programs into small computers by arranging for several program units to share a common pool of memory. This is not a recommended programming practice and is likely to become redundant with the spread of virtual-memory operating systems.

The name of a common block is an external name which must be different from all other global names, including procedure names, in the executable program. The variables and arrays stored with the block cannot be initialised in the normal way, but only in a BLOCK DATA program unit which was invented especially for this purpose.

12.1 Using Common Blocks

In most cases the best way to pass information from one program unit to another is to use the procedure argument list mechanism. This preserves the modularity and independence of procedures as much as possible. Argument lists are, however, less satisfactory in a group of procedures forming a package which have to share a large amount of information with each other. Procedure argument lists then tend to become long, cumbersome, and even inefficient. If this package of procedures is intended for general use it is quite important to keep the external interface as uncomplicated as possible. This can be achieved by using the procedure argument lists only for import of information from and export to the rest of the program, and handling the communications between one procedure in the package and another with common blocks. The user is then free to ignore the internal workings of the package.

For example, in a simple package to handle a pen-plotter you may want to provide simple procedure calls such as:

CALL PLOPEN	Initialise the plotting device
CALL SCALE(F)	Set the scaling factor to F.
CALL MOVE(X,Y)	Move the pen to position (X,Y)
CALL DRAW(X,Y)	Draw a line from the last pen position to (X,Y).

These procedures clearly have to pass information from one to another about the current pen position, scaling factor, etc. A suitable common block definition might look like this:

```
COMMON /PLOT/ OPENED, ORIGIN(2), PSCALE, NUMPEN
LOGICAL OPENED
INTEGER NUMPEN
REAL PSCALE, ORIGIN
SAVE /PLOT/
```

These specification statements would be needed in each procedure in the package.

Common block names

A program unit can access the contents of any common block by quoting its name in a COMMON statement. Common block names are always enclosed in a pair of slashes and can only be used in COMMON and SAVE statements. The common block itself has no data type and has a global name which must be distinct from the names of all program units. The name should also be distinct from all local names in each program unit which accesses the block. Each program unit can make use of any number of different common blocks. There is also a special *blank* or *unnamed* common block with unique properties (which are covered in section 12.2).

The variables and arrays within a common block do not have any global status: they are associated with items in blocks bearing the same name in other program units only by their position within the block. Thus, if in one program unit specifies:

```
COMMON /OBTUSE/ X(3)
```

and in another:

```
COMMON /OBTUSE/ A, B, C
```

then, assuming the data types are the same, X(1) corresponds to A, X(2) to B, and X(3) to C. The COMMON statements here are effectively setting up different names, or aliases, for the same set of memory locations. The data types do not have to match provided the overall length is the same, but it is generally only possible to transfer information from one program unit to another if the corresponding items have the same data type. If they do not, when one item becomes defined all names for the same location which have a different data type become undefined. There is one minor exception to this rule: information may be transferred from a *complex* variable (or array element) to two variables of type *real* (or vice versa) since these are directly associated with its real and imaginary parts.

Usually it is necessary to arrange for corresponding items to have identical data types; it also minimises confusion if the same symbolic names are used as well. The simplest way to achieve this is to use an INCLUDE statement, if your system provides one. The include-file should contain not only the COMMON statement but also all the associated type and SAVE statements which are necessary. It is, of course, still necessary to recompile every program unit which accesses the common block whenever its definition is altered significantly.

Declaring arrays

The bounds of an array can be declared in the COMMON statement itself, or in a separate *type* or DIMENSION statement, but only in one of them. Thus:

```
COMMON /DEMO/ ARRAY(5000)
DOUBLE PRECISION ARRAY
```

is exactly equivalent to:

```
COMMON /DEMO/ ARRAY
DOUBLE PRECISION ARRAY(5000)
```

or even:

```
COMMON /DEMO/ ARRAY
DOUBLE PRECISION ARRAY
DIMENSION ARRAY(5000)
```

but the verbosity of the third form has little to recommend it.

Data types

The normal data type rules apply to variables and arrays in each common block. A type statement is not required if the initial letter rule would have the required effect, but type statements are advisable, especially if the implied-type rules are anywhere affected by IMPLICIT statements. Type statements may precede or follow the COMMON statement. Similarly, the lengths of character items should be specified in a separate type statement: these cannot be specified in the COMMON statement.

Storage units

The *length* of each common block is measured in *storage units*, as described in section 5.1. In summary, integer, real and logical items occupy one numeric storage unit each; complex and double precision items occupy two each. To maximise portability, character storage units are considered incommensurate with numerical storage units. For this reason character and non-character items cannot be mixed in the same common block.

In practice this often means that two common blocks are needed to hold a particular data structure: one for the character items and one for all the others. If, in the first example, it had been necessary for the plotting package to store a plot title this would have to appear in a separate common block such as:

```
      COMMON /PLOTC/ TITLE
      CHARACTER TITLE*40
      SAVE /PLOTC/
```

It is good practice to use related names for the blocks to indicate that the character and non-character items are used in conjunction.

The length of a *named* common block must be the same in each program unit in which it appears. Obviously the easiest way to ensure this is to make the common block contents identical in each program unit. Note, however, that there is no requirement for data types to match, or for them to be listed in any particular order, provided the items are not used for information transfer, and provided the total length of the block is the same in each case. Thus these common blocks are both 2000 numerical storage units in length:

```
      COMMON /SAME/ G(1000)
      DOUBLE PRECISION G
      COMMON /SAME/ A, B, C, R(1997)
      REAL A, R
      LOGICAL B
      INTEGER C
```

Items in a common block are stored in consecutive memory locations. Unfortunately there are a few computer systems which require double precision and complex items to be stored in even-numbered storage locations: these may find it hard to cope with blocks which contain a mixture of data types. Machines with this defect can nearly always be placated by arranging for all double precision and complex items to come at the beginning of each block.

SAVE statements and common blocks

Items in common blocks may become undefined when a procedure returns control to the calling unit in the same way as local variables and arrays. This will not, however, occur in the case of the *blank* common block nor in any common block which is also declared in a program unit which is higher up the current chain of procedure calls. Since the main program unit is always at the top of the chain, any common block declared in the main program can never become undefined in this way. In all other cases it is prudent to use SAVE statements.

The individual items in common blocks cannot be specified in a SAVE statement, only the common block name itself. Thus:

```
SAVE /SAME/, /DEMO/
```

If a common block is saved in any program unit then it must be saved in all of them. The SAVE statement ought therefore to be included with the COMMON and associated type statements if INCLUDE statements are used. If the program is later modified so that the common block is also declared in the main program this will bring a SAVE statement into the main program unit, but this does no harm.

Restrictions

The dummy arguments of a procedure cannot be members of a common block nor, in a function, can the variable which has same name as the function. There are also some restrictions on the use of common block items as actual arguments of procedure calls because of the possibility of multiple definition. For example, if a procedure is defined like this:

```
SUBROUTINE SILLY(ARG)
COMMON /BLOCK/ COM
```

And the same common block is also used in the calling unit, with a common block item as the actual argument, such as:

```
PROGRAM DUMMY
```

```
          COMMON /BLOCK/ VALUE
*...
          CALL SILLY(VALUE)
```

Then both ARG and COM within the subroutine SILLY are associated with the same item, VALUE, and it is therefore illegal to assign a new value to either of them.

12.2 Blank Common Blocks

Common blocks are sometimes also used to reduce the total amount of memory used by a program by arranging for several program units to share the same set of memory locations. This is a difficult and risky procedure which should not be attempted unless all else fails.

Most Fortran systems operate a storage allocation system which is completely static: each program unit has a separate allocation of memory for its local variables and arrays. If several procedures each need to use large arrays internally, the total amount of memory occupied by the program may be rather large. If a set of procedures can be identified which are invoked in sequence, rather than one calling another, it may be feasible to reduce the total memory allocation by arranging for them to share a storage area. Each will use the same common block for their internal array space.

Named common blocks are required to have the same length in each program unit: if they are used it is necessary to work out which one needs the most storage and pad out all the others to the same length. An alternative is to the use the special *blank* (or unnamed) common block which has the useful property that it may have a different length in different program units.

In one program unit, for example, you could specify:

```
          COMMON // DUMMY(10000)
```

and in another

```
          COMPLEX SERIES(512,512), SLICE(512),
     $    EXPECT(1024)
          COMMON // SERIES, SLICE, EXPECT
```

The blank common block has two other special properties. Firstly, it cannot be initialised by a DATA statement even within a BLOCK DATA program unit (but this is not a serious limitation for a block used just for scratch storage). Secondly, items within the blank common block never become undefined as a result of a procedure exit. For this reason the blank common block cannot be specified in a SAVE statement.

12.3 COMMON Statement

A program unit may contain any number of COMMON statements, each of which can define contents for any number of different common blocks. COMMON statements are specification statements and have a general form:

```
COMMON /name/ list-of-items, /name / list-of-items ...
```

Each *name* is defined as a common block name, which has global scope. The Fortran Standard allows the name to be the same as an intrinsic function, a local variable or local array, but not that of a named constant or an intrinsic function. Each *list of items* can contain names of variables and arrays. The array name may be followed by a dimension specification provided that each array is only dimensioned once in each program unit. The comma shown before the second and subsequent block-name is optional.

The name of the blank common block is normally specified as two consecutive slashes (ignoring any intervening blanks) but if it is the first block in the statement then the pair of slashes may be omitted.

The contents of a common block are a concatenation of all the definitions for it in the program unit. Thus:

```
COMMON /ONE/ A, B, C, /TWO/ ALPHA, BETA, GAMMA
COMMON /TWO/ DELTA
```

defines two blocks, /ONE/ contains three items while /TWO/ contains four of them.

In procedures, variables which are dummy arguments or which are the same as the function name cannot appear in common blocks.

12.4 Block Data Program Units

The block data program unit is a special form of program unit which is required only if it is necessary to specify initial values for variables and arrays in named common blocks. The program unit starts with a BLOCK DATA statement, ends with an END statement, and contains only specification and DATA statements. Comment lines are also permitted. The block data program unit is not executable and it is not a procedure.

The next example initialises the items in the common block for the plotting package used in section 12.1, so that the initial pen position is at the origin, the scaling factor starts at one, and so on. Thus a suitable program unit would be:

```
      BLOCK DATA SETPLT
*SETPLT initialises the values used in the plotting
*package.
      COMMON /PLOT/ OPENED, ORIGIN(2), PSCALE, NUMPEN
      LOGICAL OPENED
      INTEGER NUMPEN
      REAL PSCALE, ORIGIN
      SAVE /PLOT/
      DATA OPENED/.FALSE./,ORIGIN/2*0.0/,PSCALE/1.0/
      DATA NUMPEN/-1/
      END
```

A block data unit can specify initial values for any number of named common blocks (blank common cannot be initialised). Each common block must be complete but it is not necessary to specify initial values for all of the items within it. There can be more than one block data program unit, but a given common block cannot appear in more than one of them.

For compatibility with Fortran 66 it is also possible to have one unnamed block data program unit in a program.

Linking block data program units

If, when linking a program, one of the modules containing a procedure is accidentally omitted, the linker is almost certain to produce an error message. But, unless additional precautions are taken, this will not occur if a block data subprogram unit is omitted. The program may even appear to work without it, but is likely to produce the wrong answer.

There is a simple way to guard against this possibility: the name of the block data unit should be specified in an EXTERNAL statement in at least some of the program units in which the common block is used. There is no harm in declaring it in all of them. This ensures that a link-time reference will be generated if any of these other program units are used. There is a slight snag to this technique if an INCLUDE statement is used to bring the common block definition into each program unit including the block data unit. In order to avoid a self-reference, the include-file should not contain the EXTERNAL statement.

Despite this slight complication, this is a simple and valuable precaution. It also makes it possible to hold block data units in object libraries and retrieve them automatically when they are required, just like all other types of subprogram unit.

Appendix A: Obsolete and Deprecated Features

None of the features covered here should be used in new software: some of them are completely obsolete; others have practical defects which make them unsuitable for use in well-structured software. These brief descriptions are provided only for the benefit of programmers who have to understand and update programs designed in earlier years.

Storage of character strings in non-character items

Before the advent of the character data type it was possible to store text in arithmetic variables and arrays, although only very limited manipulation was possible. The number of characters which could be stored in each item was entirely system-dependent. One side-effect is that many systems still allow the A format descriptor to match input/ output items of arithmetic types; this sometimes allows mismatches between data-transfer lists and format descriptors to pass undetected.

Arithmetic IF statement

This is an executable statement with the form:
IF(*arithmetic-expression*) $label_1$, $label_2$, $label_3$

It generally provides a three-way branch (but two of the labels may be identical for a two-way branch). The expression may be an integer, real or double-precision value: control is transferred to the statement attached to *label₁* if its value is negative, *label₂* if zero, or *label₃*, if positive.

ASSIGN and assigned GO TO statements

These two executable statements are normally used together. The ASSIGN statement assigns a statement label value to an integer variable. When this has been done the variable no longer has an arithmetic value. If the label is attached to an executable statement the variable can only be used in an assigned GO TO statement; if attached to a FORMAT statement the variable can only be used in a READ or WRITE statement. The general forms of these statements are:

```
ASSIGN label TO integer-variable
GO TO integer-variable,(label, label, ... label)
```

In the assigned GO TO statement the comma and the entire parenthesised list of labels is optional.

Assigned GO TO can be used to provide a linkage to and from a section of a program unit acting as an internal subroutine, but is not a very convenient or satisfactory way of doing this.

PAUSE statement

PAUSE is an executable statement which halts the program in such a way that execution can be resumed in some way by the user (or on some systems by the computer operator). The general forms of the statement are identical to those of STOP, for example:

```
       PAUSE 'NOW MOUNT THE NEXT TAPE'
or     PAUSE 54321
```

PAUSE can be replaced by one WRITE and one READ statement: this is more flexible and less system-dependent.

Alternate RETURN

The alternate RETURN mechanism can be used in subroutines (but not external functions) to arrange a transfer of control to some labelled statement on completion of a CALL statement. In order to use it the arguments of the CALL statement must include a list of labels, each preceded by an asterisk. These labels are attached to points in the calling program unit at which execution may resume after the CALL statement is executed. For example:

```
       CALL BAD(X, Y, Z, *150, *220, *390)
```

The corresponding subroutine statement will have asterisks as dummy arguments for each label specification:

```
       SUBROUTINE BAD(A, B, C, *, *, *)
```

The return point depends on the value of an integer expression given in the RETURN statement. Thus:

will cause execution to be resumed at the statement attached to the second label argument, 220 in this case. If the value of the integer expression in the RETURN statement is not in the range 1 to *n* (where there are *n* label arguments) or a plain RETURN statement is executed, then execution resumes at the statement after the CALL in the usual way.

The mechanism can be used for error-handling but is not very flexible as information cannot be passed through more than one procedure level. It is better to use an integer argument to return a status value and use that with an IF (or even a computed GO TO) statement in the calling program.

ENTRY statement

ENTRY statements can be used to specify additional entry points in external functions and subroutines. ENTRY is a non-executable statement which has the same form as a SUBROUTINE statement. An ENTRY statement may be used at any point in a procedure but all specification statements relating to its dummy arguments must appear in the appropriate place with the other specification statements. If the main entry point is a SUBROUTINE statement than all alternative entry points can be called in the same way as subroutines; if it is a FUNCTION statement then all alternative entry point names can be used as functions. If the main entry point is a *character* function then all the alternative entry points must also have that type. Alternative entry points may have different lists of dummy arguments; it is up to the user to ensure that all those returning information to the calling program are properly defined before exit.

The rules for the ENTRY statement are necessarily complicated so it is easy to make mistakes. It is generally better, or at least less unsatisfactory, to use a set of separate procedures which share information using common blocks.

EQUIVALENCE statement

EQUIVALENCE is a specification statement which causes two or more items (variables or arrays) to be associated with each other, i.e. to correspond to the same area of memory. Character items can only be associated with other character items; otherwise the data types do not have to match. As with common blocks, however, transfer of information is only permitted via associated items if their data types match. A special exception is made for a complex item which is associated with two real ones.

EQUIVALENCE statements can be used fairly safely to provide a simple variable name as an alias for a particular array element or to associate a character variable with an array of the same length. For example:

```
CHARACTER STRING*80, ARRAY(80)*1
EQUIVALENCE (STRING, ARRAY)
```

This slightly simplifies access to a single character in the string as the form ARRAY(K) can be used instead of STRING(K:K).

The general form of the statement is:

```
EQUIVALENCE ( v, v, ... v ), ( v, v, ... v ), ...
```

where each *v* is a variable, array, array element, or substring. Dummy arguments of procedures (and variables which are external function names) cannot appear. An array name without subscripts refers to the first element of the array. It is illegal to associate two or more elements of the same array, directly or indirectly, or do anything which conflicts with the storage sequence rules. Variables and arrays in common blocks can appear in EQUIVALENCE statements but this has the effect of bringing all the associated items into the block. They can be used to extend the contents of the block upwards, subject to the rules for common block length, but not downwards.

Although the EQUIVALENCE statement does have a few legitimate uses it is usually encountered in programs where the rules of Fortran are broken to obtain some special effect. Programs which do this are rarely portable.

Specific names of intrinsic functions

Specific names should be used instead of the generic name of an intrinsic function only if the name is to be the actual argument of a procedure call; the name then must also be declared in an INTRINSIC statement. The following intrinsic functions cannot be used in this way, and their specific names are therefore completely obsolete.

Obsolete specific name	Preferred generic form
IFIX, IDINT	INT
FLOAT, SNGL	REAL
MAX0, AMAX1, DMAX1,	MAX
AMAX0, MAX1	MAX*
MIN0, AMIN1, DMIN1	MIN
AMIN0, MIN1	MIN*

* The functions AMAX0, MAX1, AMIN0 and MIN1 which have a data type different from that of their arguments can only be replaced by appropriate type conversion functions in addition to MAX or MIN.

PRINT statement and READ (simplified form)

The PRINT statement can produce formatted or list-directed output on the standard pre-connected output file. Thus:

```
PRINT fmt, data-list
```

is exactly equivalent to:

```
WRITE(*, fmt) data-list
```

The PRINT statement is limited in its functionality and misleading, since there is no necessity for its output to appear in printed form.

In a similar way there is a simplified form of READ statement:

```
READ fmt, data-list
```

which is exactly equivalent to:

```
READ(*, fmt) data-list
```

The END FILE statement

The END FILE statement has the same general forms as REWIND and BACKSPACE:

```
END FILE(UNIT=unit, ERR=label, IOSTAT=int-var)
END FILE unit
```

It appends a special 'end-file' record to a sequential file which is designed to trigger the end-of-file detection mechanism on subsequent input. No further records can be written to the file after this end-file record, i.e. the next operation must be CLOSE, REWIND or BACKSPACE.

The statement seems to be superfluous on almost all current systems since they can detect the end of an input file without its aid.

The Fortran Standard requires that the end-file record be treated as a physical record, so that after an end-of-file condition has been detected an explicit BACKSPACE operation is required before any new data records are appended. This notion is somewhat artificial and not all systems implement it correctly. This is one of the few cases where a deliberate departure from the Fortran Standard can enhance portability.

Obsolete format descriptors

The data descriptor D$w.d$ is exactly equivalent to E$w.d$ on input; on output it is similar except that the exponent will use the letter D instead of E. Real and double precision data items can be read equally well by D, E, F or G descriptors.

The format descriptor

```
nHstring
```

is exactly equivalent to

```
'string'
```

(where *n* is an unsigned integer constant giving the length of the string). When it is used with a formatted WRITE statement the string is copied to the output record. The nH form does not require apostrophes to be doubled within the string but does require an accurate character count.

APPENDIX B: Summary of Subset Differences

The list below summarises features lacking in Subset Fortran. Note, however, that many systems which can only claim Subset conformance actually provide almost all of the features of Full Fortran 77.

Character set and layout

The character set does not contain the currency symbol or colon. Only nine continuation lines are allowed, and comments are not permitted within a set of continuation lines. There are no BLOCK DATA program units.

Data types and arrays

There are only four data types: double precision and complex are omitted. Arrays can have no more than 3 dimensions. Lower bounds cannot be specified; upper bounds can only be specified by integer constants (or variables in the case of arrays which are dummy arguments). The PARAMETER statement cannot be used. The SAVE statement can only be used with a list of common blocks. DATA statements must appear before all statement function and executable statements; DATA statements cannot use implied-DO loops and do not provide automatic type conversion.

Control statements

The loop control variable in a DO statement must have integer type; the loop limit and step-size parameters must be integer constants or variables. The control item in computed GO TO must be an integer variable.

Input/output

CLOSE, INQUIRE and PRINT statements are omitted, as are list-directed I/O, formatted direct-access files, and ERR= identifiers. The unit identifier must not be preceded by UNIT= and must be an integer constant or variable; the format identifier must not be preceded by FMT= and must be the label of a FORMAT statement. WRITE statements cannot have expressions in their output lists. The OPEN statement can only be used to open direct-access files: these cannot be named, and the statement must have the form:

OPEN(UNIT=*constant*, ACCESS='DIRECT', RECL =*constant*)

Format descriptors G, T, TL, TR, S, SP, SS and : are not permitted nor are the forms I*w.m*, D*w.d*. Only three levels of parentheses are allowed.

Miscellaneous

Character substrings and the concatenation operator are omitted. Character functions cannot be used and the intrinsic functions LEN, CHAR and INDEX are omitted. Dummy argument character items must have fixed length.

There are no generic names for arithmetic intrinsic functions. The logical operators .EQV. and .NEQV. are absent.

There is no ENTRY statement or alternate RETURN.

Appendix C: List of Intrinsic Functions

The table below shows the number of arguments for each function and what data types are permitted. When more than one argument is allowed all must have the same data type.

The data type codes are:

    I   Integer,   Cx Complex
    R Real,   Ch Character
    D Double precision, L   Logical

The data type that the function returns is shown on the left; an asterisk here indicates that it has the same data type as the arguments.

R =	ABS(Cx)	Takes the modulus of a complex number (i.e. the square-root of the sum of the squares of the two components).
★ =	ABS(IRD)	Absolute value of a number (i.e. it changes the sign if negative).
★ =	ACOS(RD)	Arc-cosine; the result is in the range 0 to $+\pi$.
R =	AIMAG(Cx)	Extracts the imaginary component of a complex number. Use REAL to extract the real component.
★ =	AINT(RD)	Truncates the fractional part (i.e. as does INT) but preserves the data type.
★ =	ANINT(RD)	Rounds to the nearest whole number.
★ =	ASIN(RD)	Arc-sine; the result is in the range $-\pi/2$ to $+\pi/2$.
★ =	ATAN(RD)	Arc-tangent; the result is in the range $-\pi/2$ to $+\pi/2$.
★ =	ATAN2(RD,RD)	Arc-tangent of A_1/A_2 resolved into the correct quadrant, the result is in the range $-\pi$ to $+\pi$. It is an error to have both arguments zero.
Ch =	CHAR(I)	Returns Nth character in local character code table.

Cx =	CMPLX(IRDCx)	Converts to complex.
Cx =	CMPLX(IRD,IRD)	Converts to complex.
Cx =	CONJG(Cx)	Computes the complex conjugate of a complex number.
★ =	COS(RDCx)	Cosine of the angle in radians.
★ =	COSH(RD)	Hyperbolic cosine.
D =	DBLE(IRDCx)	Converts to double precision.
★ =	DIM(IRD,IRD)	Returns the positive difference of A_1 and A_2, i.e. if $A_1 > A_2$ it returns $(A_1 - A_2)$, otherwise zero.
D =	DPROD(R,R)	Computes the double precision product of two real values.
★ =	EXP(RDCx)	Returns the exponential, i.e. e to the power of the argument. This is the inverse of the natural logarithm.
I =	ICHAR(Ch)	Returns position of first character of the string in the local character code table.
I =	INDEX(Ch,Ch)	Searches first string and returns position of second string within it, otherwise zero.
I =	INT(IRDCx)	Converts to integer by truncation.
I =	LEN(Ch)	Returns length of the character argument.
L =	LGE(Ch,Ch)	Lexical comparison using ASCII character code: returns *true* if $A_1 \geq A_2$.
L =	LGT(Ch,Ch)	Lexical comparison using ASCII character code: returns *true* if $A_1 > A_2$.
L =	LLE(Ch,Ch)	Lexical comparison using ASCII character code: returns *true* if $A_1 \leq A_2$.
L =	LLT(Ch,Ch)	Lexical comparison using ASCII character code: returns *true* if $A_1 < A_2$.
★ =	LOG(RDCx)	Natural logarithm, i.e. log to base e (where e = 2.718281828...).
★ =	LOG10(RD)	Logarithm to base 10.
★ =	MAX(IRD,IRD,...)	Returns the largest of its arguments.
★ =	MIN(IRD,IRD,...)	Returns the smallest of its arguments.
★ =	MOD(IRD,IRD)	Returns A_1 modulo A_2, i.e. the remainder after dividing A_1 by A_2.
I =	NINT(RD)	Converts to integer by rounding to the nearest whole number.
R =	REAL(IRDCx)	Converts to real.

★ =	SIGN(IRD,IRD)	Performs sign transfer: if A_1 is negative the result is $-A_1$, if A_2 is zero or positive the result is A_1.
★ =	SIN(RDCx)	Sine of the angle in radians.
★ =	SINH(RD)	Hyperbolic sine.
★ =	SQRT(RDCx)	Square root.
★ =	TAN(RD)	Tangent of the angle in radians.
★ =	TANH(RD)	Hyperbolic tangent.

Specific names of generic functions

Specific names are still needed when the function name is used as the actual argument of another procedure. The specific name must then also be declared in the INSTRINSIC statement. This table lists all the specific names which are still useful in Fortran 77. The other functions either do not have generic names or cannot be passed as actual arguments.

Generic name	Specific names			
	Integer	Real	Double precision	Complex
ABS	IABS	ABS	DABS	CABS
ACOS		ACOS	DACOS	
AINT		AINT	DINT	
ANINT		AINT	DNINT	
ASIN		ASIN	DASIN	
ATAN		ATAN	DATAN	
ATAN2		ATAN2	DATAN2	
COS		COS	DCOS	CCOS
COSH		COSH	DCOSH	
DIM	IDIM	DIM	DDIM	
EXP		EXP	DEXP	CEXP
LOG		ALOG	DLOG	CLOG
LOG10		ALOG10	DLOG10	
MOD	MOD	AMOD	DMOD	
NINT		NINT	IDNINT	
SIGN	ISIGN	SIGN	DSIGN	
SIN		SIN	DSIN	CSIN
SINH		SINH	DSINH	
SQRT		SQRT	DSQRT	CSQRT
TAN		TAN	DTAN	
TANH		TANH	DTANH	

Index

Index

The page numbers of the principal or defining references are given in **bold**.

ANSI Standard   2
Arguments, procedure   **96–106**
Arithmetic data types   **38**
Array   **52–53**, 101–104, 158
ASCII character set   27, **75**
ASSIGN statement   **164**
Assignment statement
   arithmetic   **65**
   character   **70**
   logical   **78**

BACKSPACE statement   116, **148**
Bit-wise logic   5, **60**
Blank character   **26**, 45, 134, 141, 145
Blank common block   161
BLOCK DATA statement   31, **162**
Branches   79, **86**

CALL statement   93, 96, **107**
Carriage-control characters   **27**, 137
Character set, Fortran   **26**
CHARACTER statement   **46**
Character type   **40**, 44, 67–76, 104, 152
CLOSE statement   114, **142**
Collating sequence   **75**
Comment lines   **29**
Common blocks   95, **156–163**, 167
COMMON statement   **162**
Compiling   19, **21**
Complex type   **39**, 42, 44
Constant expression   50, **60**
Constants   **42–45**, 48
Continuation lines   **28**
CONTINUE statement   **83**
Currency symbol   **27–28**

DATA statement   **150–155**, 162
Data type conversions   58, 63, 71, 120
Data types   **38–45**
DIMENSION statement   52
Direct-access files   **116**, 119–120, 146
DO statement   4, 5, 54, **82–85**
DO-loops, implied   147, 153
Double precision type   **39**, 42, 44

END DO statement   4
END FILE statement   168
END statement   29, 33, **35**, 93
End-of-file detection   **123–125**, 146, 168
ENTRY statement   **166**
EQUIVALENCE statement   **166**
Error handling   22, 24, 123
Executable image   **19**
Execution sequence   **33**
Expressions
  arithmetic   **55–60**
  character   50, **69**
  constant   50, **60**
  logical   **76–78**
  relational   **73–76**
EXTERNAL statement   **111**, 163

Files
  external   113, **117**
  internal   113, **120**
Format
  descriptors   **128–135**, 169
  specifications   118, **125**, 146
FORMAT statement   **127**
Formatted files   **115**, 117, 120
Fortran 8x   **3**, 33
FUNCTION statement   96, **108–109**
Functions
  external   **93**
  intrinsic   35, 61–65, 71–73, 89, **172–174**
  statement   **90**

GO TO statements   85, **86**, 164

I/O units   **114**, 140
IF statements   80, **85**, 164
IMPLICIT statement   5, **47**

178

INCLUDE statement **5**, 21, 51, 92, 158
Initialisation **151–152**
INQUIRE statement 114, **142**
Integer type **38**, 42
Internal files **113**, 120
Intrinsic functions 89, **172–174**
   arithmetic **61–65**
   character **71–73**
INTRINSIC statement **111**, 174

Keywords 27, 138

Labels, statement **29**, 85, 86, 124, 126
Libraries **22**
Linking **22**, 163
List-directed formatting 117, **135**
Logical type **40**, 42, 44
Loops **79**
Lower-case letters 27, 76

Names, symbolic 5, **33**, 45

OPEN statement 114, **139**
Operators 57, 74, 77

PARAMETER statement **50**, 67, 150
PAUSE statement **165**
Portability 4, 21, 26, 33, 42, 71, 75, 111, 116, 119, 122, 138, 140, 167, 169
Pre-connected files **122**
PRINT statement **168**
Printing **137**
Procedures 31, **89**, 93, 153
PROGRAM statement **35**
Program units 20, **30**, 162

READ statement **145–148**, 168
Real type **39**, 43
Records **115**
Relational expressions **73–76**
Reserved words **34**
RETURN statement 93, **107**, 148, 165

SAVE statement 93, **110**, 153, 160
Sequential files **116**
Source code **20**
Space character **26**, 45, 134, 141, 145

Statement function statement **90**
Statement layout **27**
  ordering rules **32**
Statements, executable and non-executable **32**
STOP statement **33, 87**
Storage sequence, array **54**
  units **41**, 159
SUBROUTINE statement **96, 106**
Subset Fortran 2, **170**
Substrings, character **68**, 99, 152

Terminal input/output **122–123**, 138
Text files **117**, 122
Type conversions **63**, 120
Type statements **46**

Undefined values **150**
Unformatted files **115–119**

Variables **51**

WRITE statement **145–148**